EAST RIDING

TALES FROM THE EAST RIDING

MARTIN LIMON

TEMPUS

Frontispiece: John Paul Jones, American naval hero, loses his temper with one of his own crew during a sea battle off Flamborough Head.

First published 2006

Tempus Publishing Limited
The Mill, Brimscombe Port,
Stroud, Gloucestershire, GL5 2QG
www.tempus-publishing.com

British Library Cataloguing in Publication Data.
A catalogue record for this book is available from the British Library.

ISBN 0 7524 4038 1

Typesetting and origination by Tempus Publishing Limited.
Printed in Great Britain.

Contents

Acknowledgements

In preparing these local history features for publication I would like to give a special thanks to the following people: The staff of East Riding Archives Service , Beverley, Archives Service of Kingston upon Hull City Council, Beverley Local Studies Library and Hull Local Studies Library; Bartoline Ltd, Beverley; Nick Cox; John Ridyard; Nick Wright; Robert Preedy; Dean Mosher; Colin Westley; John Richardson; Paula Gentil, Keeper of Archaeology Hull and East Riding Museum; The Ken Hoole Centre, Darlington; Jon Myler; The Heritage Centre, BAE Systems, Brough.

Introduction

This collection of local history tales has its origins in a Hull University course, taken during my degree studies, taught by distinguished historian Ken McMahon, over thirty years ago. Called 'The Corporate Boroughs of Yorkshire' this fascinating introduction to local history provided me with a stimulus to further research both in my career as a history teacher and for subsequent writing.

A lot can happen in three years and after my self-published book on Wawne Ferry came articles for *Down Your Way* magazine, *Flashback* and, most importantly, for the *East Riding Gazette* (2003-4). This impressive, if short-lived, free newspaper gave me the opportunity to write a series of local history features on topics that interested me from the industrialist Gordon Armstrong to the story of Beverley Races. These nine features for the *East Riding Gazette*, published between March and September 2004, appear again in this book. Articles for other magazines, like the *Yorkshire Ridings Magazine*, followed: the first being 'When Ealing Studios Came to East Yorkshire' - the story of the Robert Donat's film *Lease of Life*. The publication of this book has given me the opportunity to bring these stories together in one volume and also to add new and previously unpublished material. I would like to take this opportunity to thank the numerous individuals and organisations that have assisted in the research for these articles or provided images to accompany them. Thanks also to David Buxton of Tempus Publishing for his constant encouragement and advice and to my wife Lynne and my sons Marc and Tim for their enthusiastic support of this venture.

Martin Limon
Thearne,
Beverley
East Yorkshire.
August 2006

I

Pax Romana: Roman East Yorkshire

For over three hundred years East Yorkshire was part of one of the greatest empires the world has ever known, The Roman Empire. Beginning around AD 70 the Roman way of life transformed the landscape of this part of the country with roads, towns and villas.

The Roman conquest of Britain had begun in AD 43 when Emperor Claudius sent an army under the command of Aulus Plautius. The Romans rapidly conquered the south-east of the island and by AD 71 their northern frontier lay along the south bank of the River Humber. In that year, prompted by a rebellion of one of the tribes of northern Britain, the Brigantes, the Romans crossed the river and began the incorporation of East Yorkshire and other areas of northern Britain into the empire. The East Riding was already inhabited by the Celtic people known as the Parisi tribe and, unlike the Brigantes, it seems that that these were peaceful and did not give the Romans trouble.

The capital of the Parisi was at Brough and this became the Roman military base called Petuaria. A Roman fort was first established here in 71 AD under the command of Petilus Cerialis This fortress covered about 4.5 acres and from here communications by ferry would have been established via Brough Haven to Winteringham and then south by the Roman road known as Ermine Street to Lincoln. From Brough another Roman road led north through present-day South Cave to Market Weighton. From here the road branched with one route leading to the Roman legionary fortress of Eboracum (York) and another continuing north across the Yorkshire Wolds to Malton. Here another Roman military base and, subsequently a town, were established. Other minor Roman roads were also established some of which followed existing routeways; there is evidence, for example, of a stone-built Roman ford across the River Hull at Wawne to link the route into Holderness.

We know a little about Petuaria from both ancient documents and from archaeological excavations in the 1930s. Ptolemy's 'Geography', written in the early second century AD, mentions both the Parisi and the town of Petuaria. In the century after it was established, Petuaria seems to have grown in importance. An inscription on a stone slab discovered in 1937 records how a magistrate of the town, Marcus Ulpius Januarius, from his own funds, donated a new stage for its theatre. The inscription was in honour of the Emperor Antoninus Pius (AD 138-161) and records the civic status of the town as a vicus. Thus, by the early second century Petuaria must have been of sufficient wealth and importance to earn some of the trappings of Roman civilisation. From the evidence of other Roman town sites we know that permanent theatres began to be constructed, consisting of an auditorium with curved rows of seats rising in tiers, an arena or orchestra, a raised stage and a back wall or scaena. The theatre was usually unroofed (but could be protected from the weather by awnings) and in Roman Britain it would probably have been constructed of wood. Elsewhere in the empire stone-built theatres were more common. Theatrical performances of Greek tragedies and comedies were popular with the educated social classes. Women were not allowed on stage and so the actors wore masks to indicate their roles, male or female.

During the reign of Emperor Hadrian (AD 117-138) the town's ramparts and a stockade were built and strengthened by the creation of a 9ft thick stone wall some forty years later during the reign of Antonius Pius. Excavations from the 1930s indicate that by AD 270 Petuaria had become a fairly prosperous place and had grown to about 12 acres in size. In Roman times Brough Haven extended north from the Humber estuary to the western side of the town and archaeological investigations suggest that a quay was constructed here for the loading and unloading of boats from Winteringham and perhaps further afield.

There are other indications of the Roman occupation of East Yorkshire and the trade they engaged in. South Cave lay on the Roman road between Petuaria and Market Weighton and in 1890 a block of lead from Roman times, weighing over 61 kg, was found there. The ingot's Latin inscription indicates that it had come from the mines of Julius Protus of Lutudae (probably Derbyshire). Lead was used extensively during Roman times in the building trade for water pipes, bath linings, roofing and cisterns as well as for coffins, containers for cremated remains and smaller objects such as weights. Other evidence (for example, at Holme on Spalding Moor) indicates increasing economic activity in areas like pottery manufacture. It was normal for pottery-like simple earthenware vessels to be supplied to fairly local markets as it was a bulky and fragile commodity to transport over long distances.

The Roman occupation seems also to have had an impact on farming activity in East Yorkshire. The evidence suggests that there was a shift from pastoral farming to cereal production as military garrisons and urban populations, like those at Petuaria and Eboracum, needed large amounts of grain (mainly for making bread). Over time it is likely that the peace and prosperity brought by the Roman occupation led to improved living standards for the native population, many of whom seem to have adopted the Roman way of life and became Romanised Britons. This can be seen at the sites of Roman villas (a term which has been used to describe almost any Roman house in the countryside) in East Yorkshire including Welton, Brantingham and Rudston. By the fourth century many of East Yorkshire's Roman villas contained the luxury features associated with Roman civilisation: mosaic floors, underfloor heating, wall decoration and bath-houses.

A good example of a Roman villa has been identified at Rudston, six miles west of Bridlington. Excavations suggest that the villa was begun around the end of the first century AD (the earliest coin found has been dated to AD 81-96) on the site of an earlier Iron Age farmstead. Archaeological investigation showed that Rudston had three ranges of buildings around a courtyard and that one of these was the bath suite. Bathing was a social occasion and bath suites contained a series of interlinked rooms; at Rudston there was a warm room, a hot room and a cold plunge bath. The idea was to rub olive oil into the skin, get up a good sweat in the hot room and then to scrape off the oil, sweat and dirt using a curved instrument called a strigil. Participants would then take a refreshing dip in the cold plunge bath! The bath suite at Rudston was equipped with underfloor heating (hypocausts) where hot air from a furnace passed through the air spaces beneath the floor with gases and heat escaping through flues in the walls. The floor was supported on stacks of tiles.

This roundel from the charioteer mosaic found at Rudston Villa shows the head of Spring with a swallow on her shoulder. (courtesy Hull and East Riding Museum)

Both the main living quarters and the bath suite of Rudston villa were decorated with mosaic floors indicating just how prosperous the estate was by the early fourth century. A mosaic floor of patterns or pictures was made of small cubes of coloured stone called tesserae; most of these would have been made from stone found locally although the browns and yellows may have been brought in from further afield. At Rudston, archaeologists found a storeroom with a large stock of ready-to-use and unfinished tesserae.

The mosaic floors from Rudston (now to be found in Hull's Archeological Museum) include some interesting examples of the mosaic-maker's art. The best of the mosaics, the Charioteer, was discovered in 1971 in what archaeologists believed was the main living quarters of the villa. This skillfully executed mosaic shows a Roman circus chariot with the charioteer holding a palm and a wreath (symbols of victory). In the four corners of the mosaic are designs representing the four seasons, a particular favourite of mosaic builders. The mosaics in the bath suite however seem to have been assembled later, possibly in the mid- to late-fourth century. By this time there may have been a growing shortage of skilled mosaic builders since the Venus mosaic shows the figure of Venus with oddly shaped limbs. In comparison to the Charioteer mosaic the Venus mosaic is amateurish in design and may have been the work of a semi-skilled British craftsman.

The poor execution of the Venus mosaic may be an indication of the problems facing the Roman Empire by the end of the fourth century AD, including a scarcity of skilled labour. The economy of the empire weakened due to a variety of factors including disease, the scarcity

Above: There is evidence of Roman pottery manufacture at Holme on Spalding Moor in East Yorkshire. Simple earthenware vessels like these would have been supplied to local markets as it was a bulky and fragile commodity to transport over long distances.

Opposite above: The Venus mosaic found in the bath suite of Rudston villa. The figure has oddly shaped limbs and may have been the work of a semi-skilled craftsman made during the latter part of Roman rule in Britain. (courtsey Hull and East Riding Museum)

Opposite below: The present-day Burrs playing field in Brough covers about a third of the site of the old Roman town of Petuaria. It was excavated in the 1930s to a depth of about five feet.

of slaves, the debasement of the coinage and increased taxation. It was also racked by political instability and became increasingly unable to defend itself from the menace of barbarian tribes from outside. Evidence from Petuaria for example suggests a decline in the town's fortunes by the late fourth century but the strengthening of the town's walls by the addition of external towers. This may be an indication of the increasing threat from Germanic tribesmen of northern Europe.

With the decline and eventual collapse of centralised Roman power, provinces such as Britain were abandoned by the end of the fourth century and left to defend themselves against external attack. Without the support of a strong Roman army it seems that this was a challenge the local inhabitants were ill equipped to meet. Although lack of evidence means that we do not know when, precisely, East Yorkshire's villas were abandoned, the latest coin found at Rudston Villa is from the time of Constantine' in the late fourth century.

2

Clash of Arms: Stamford Bridge and the Rout of the Norsemen

From their schooldays most people remember being taught about the events of 1066 and in particular the Battle of Hastings and the Norman Conquest of England that followed it. However the year1066 saw three major battles in England: Fulford, Stamford Bridge and Hastings. It was the second of these, at Stamford Bridge on the fringe of East Yorkshire, which was to influence the outcome of the Battle of Hastings and change the course of English history.

The village of Stamford Bridge, about seven miles east ofYork on the River Derwent, has long been an important place for travellers. During Roman times sandstone had been laid on the riverbed to create a ford at the place where roads running north to south and east to west met. By the eleventh century the Roman ford, it would seem, had been supplemented by a narrow timber bridge. It was to this strategic crossing place that the armies of Harold Godwinsson, King of England since early January 1066, and Harald Hardrada, King of Norway, moved on Monday 25 September 1066.

The Battle of Stamford Bridge that followed was the result of events set in chain by the death of the English king Edward the Confessor on the 5 January 1066. His successor Harold Godwinsson, Earl of Wessex, was not of royal descent and there were other claimants prepared to resist his *coup d'etat* notably William, Duke of Normandy and Harald Hardrada, King of Norway.

Hardrada was a ruthless and murderous Norse warrior and was aided in his invasion plans by the English king's renegade brother, Earl Tostig. Gathering a large fleet and army (said to number over 300 ships and 10,000 troops) they attacked the Yorkshire coast and in what we think of as typical Viking fashion burned and plundered Scarborough on or around the 15 September 1066. By the 18 September they had navigated the Humber and the Ouse landing at Riccall south of York, the prize which Hardrada and Tostig clearly had in mind. They were opposed by an English force, led by earls Morcar and Edwin, that moved south to meet them.

On Wednesday 20 September the two sides clashed at Fulford and in a bloody encounter the Norsemen were victorious. Rather than share the fate of Scarborough the people of York then offered to surrender and to ensure good faith negotiated an exchange of hostages with the Norwegians. It would appear that Stamford Bridge was chosen as the rendezvous point where the hostage exchange and the re-provisioning of Hardrada's army would take place on Monday 25 September 1066.

According to contemporary sources of these events, Hardrada and his troops then withdrew to their fleet at Riccall. What is not clear is the reason for the delay between the Battle of Fulford

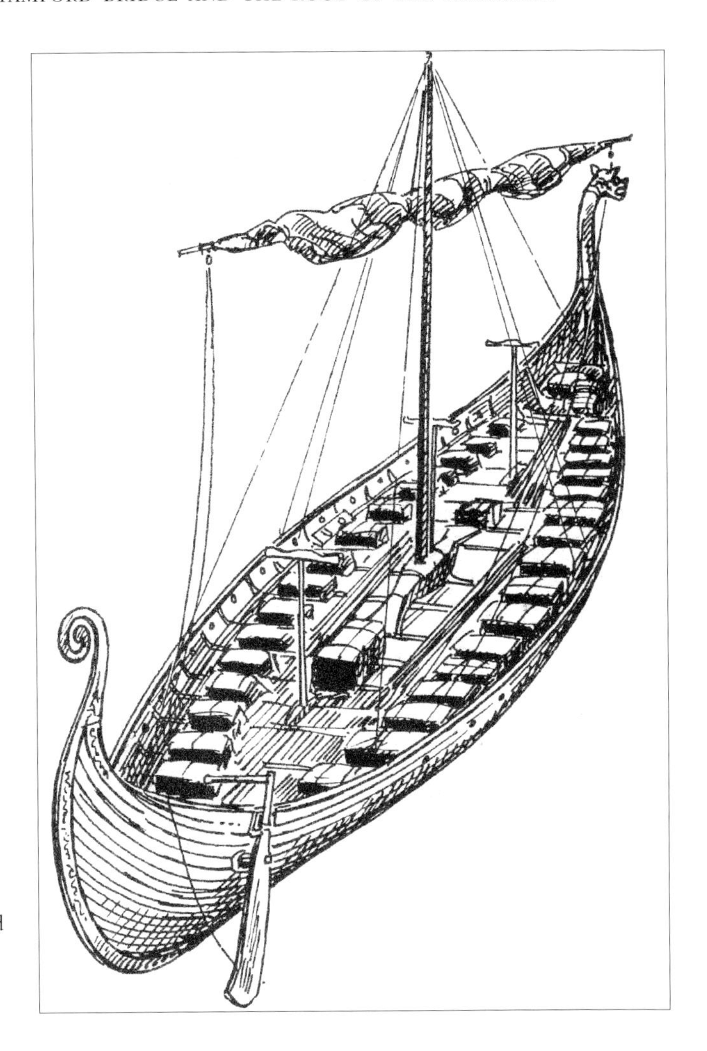

In September 1066 Hardrada's ships navigated the Humber and the Ouse and landed at Riccall south of York. (courtesy *The Times*)

(Wednesday 20 September) and the exchange of hostages (Monday 25 September) and why Stamford Bridge was chosen as the rendezvous point. The choice of Stamford Bridge, although at the junction of important routes, appears to make little military sense for Riccall was some twelve miles away. In the event Hardrada's brash overconfidence after the Battle of Fulford, his poor military intelligence and his decision to use Stamford Bridge for the hostage exchange and his re-provisioning were to prove disastrous to his cause.

Judged by their almost leisurely reactions both Hardrada and Tostig seem to have miscalculated the likely response of King Harold to their attacks in Yorkshire. Perhaps they assumed that he would remain inactive in the south awaiting the invasion by Duke William from Normandy and thus give them time to consolidate their earlier success. In the event Harold's reaction to the news from the north was swift and decisive. By the 20 September, the same day as the Battle of Fulford, Harold's newly raised Saxon army began an epic journey north and covered the 185 miles from London to Yorkshire in just four days, gathering other troops along the way. By the night of the 24/25 September they were in Tadcaster and the following day moved on to York where, it seemed, Harold learned of the rendezvous at Stamford Bridge.

Memorial to the battle of Stamford Bridge.

Part of the problem in understanding exactly what happened next lies in the inadequacy of contemporary sources covering these events. From original manuscripts (now lost) different versions of the 'Anglo-Saxon Chronicle' were compiled in several religious houses during the eleventh and twelfth centuries. These suggest that on arriving at Stamford Bridge, King Harold had the advantage of surprise over the Norsemen and such was the speed of the Saxon attack that Hardrada did not have enough time to prepare. However, for much of the detail of the battle itself historians have been forced to rely on a collection of Norse Sagas written two hundred years later by Snorri Sturlasson, an Icelandic scholar. Sturlasson compiled these sagas from stories passed down by word of mouth and they seem to be a mix of fact and fiction.

However, from the available evidence it seems that most of the fighting took place beyond the bridge, on the southern bank of the River Derwent, within the area known as Battle Flats. At what point Hardrada became aware of Harold's presence is unclear. From the evidence of the Norse Sagas it seems that Hardrada and Tostig had barely reached Stamford Bridge when they saw 'a great cloud of dust and under it bright shields and shining mail'.

Although Harold and his elite force of Housecarls probably arrived on horseback, the bulk of his soldiers, the Fyrd, would have been on foot. These part-time fighters were summoned from

The Swordsman Inn, Stamford Bridge. The pub sign depicts a lone Viking holding back the Saxon army before being killed by a spear thrust from under the bridge. The popular idea that Vikings wore horned helmets is probably a myth.

their farm work to fight for their king as and when the need arose. The Housecarls would have dismounted to fight for it is thought that all Saxon and Norse troops fought on foot during this period. The troops of Hardrada and Tostig were a mix of Norwegians, Flemings and Scots. Both sides would have used similar weapons at Stamford Bridge including spears (used both for throwing and thrusting), bows, swords and battle-axes. Harold's Housecarls were particularly famous for the skilled use of the battle-axe in hand-to-hand combat. Many, if not all, troops carried a shield that could be formed into a shield wall for both defence and attack.

Hardrada may have had time to deploy some of his men beyond the river to delay the Saxon advance. According to local legend, supported by some historical sources, one heroic Norwegian single-handedly blocked the narrow wooden bridge preventing the Saxons from crossing it until he was killed by a spear thrust from underneath.

If the Norse Sagas are to be believed then Hardrada and his men were ill-prepared to meet the tide of Saxon housecarls and other troops who swept across the river and up the hill to meet them on Battle Flats. Presumably unaware of Harold's presence in the neighbourhood, Hardrada had left a third of his men behind with his longships at Riccall, 12 miles away. Furthermore, according to the sagas at least, the day was hot and sunny and those who set out for Stamford

Bridge 'left behind their mailshirts' and only took their shields, helmets spears and swords. The account of Snorri Sturlasson claims that when Hardrada did become aware of the Saxon army he dispatched horsemen to summon the remainder of the Viking troops at Riccall.

The Sagas tell that by the time reinforcements arrived a large number of the Norwegians were already dead. In the manner of the Sagas the death of Hardrada himself was recorded in heroic style. According to Sturlasson's account the king tried to rally the men around his raven banner through personal courage and 'gripped the hilt of his sword with both hands and hewed on both sides ... and killed many men'. Yet in the end the Saxon numerical superiority began to tell and Hardrada received 'a wound in the front of his throat so that blood straightaway gushed from his mouth' and so died along with all those who stood near him. Sturlasson then records that King Harold offered his brother a truce but when this was refused the fighting continued and Tostig too was killed. From Sturlasson's account we also learn that before the Norwegians were overcome their reinforcements from Riccall arrived on the scene. Although exhausted after their long march Sturlasson claims they gave a good account of themselves until superior Saxon numbers brought the battle to its inevitable conclusion.

By comparison, the various versions of the 'Anglo-Saxon Chronicle' tell us little of the actual battle against the Vikings other than King Harold 'came upon them unawares beyond the bridge', that the fighting went on until late in the day, and that Hardrada and Tostig were both killed along with countless English and Norwegians. One version of the Chronicle states that the surviving Norwegians then took flight back to their ships but that the English 'attacked them fiercely as they pursued them ... so that few survived'. The Chronicler also tells us that those left aboard the ships, including Hardrada's son Olaf, were allowed to live after swearing oaths promising future peace with Harold. They were then allowed to leave for Norway aboard twenty-four of their own ships while leaving the rest behind as spoils of war for the Saxons.

The Battle of Stamford Bridge thus ended in a rout of the Norsemen and a huge though indeterminate loss of life, particularly so for the invaders. The writings of Orderic Vitalis (1075-1142) provide a macabre postscript to the battle itself as he records. 'the field of battle may easily be discovered by travellers as great heaps of the bones of the slain lie there to this day, memorials of the prodigious numbers which fell on both sides'. The bodies of Tostig and Hardrada fared somewhat better: it is said that Hardrada's body was later recovered and shipped back to Trondheim in Norway while Tostig received a Christian burial in York.

Stamford Bridge was a decisive victory for Harold and his Saxon army and showed that he was a highly competent commander and that his troops, especially the Housecarls, were an effective fighting force capable of moving swiftly over great distances. Although discussion of the importance of Stamford Bridge tends to focus on its significance for the Battle of Hastings and the fate of England's Saxon rulers, the battle of September 25 1066 also marked the final Norse invasion of England. The ambitions of the Norwegians to rule the country really came to an end with the death of Hardrada.

Yet while King Harold had emerged triumphant his was to be a hollow victory since within days news was brought of Duke William's invasion from Normandy. By moving north to deal with Hardrada and Tostig, Harold was unable to oppose the Norman landing on the south coast. Furthermore the losses that the Saxons endured at Stamford Bridge forced Harold to confront William three weeks later with an army that was both weaker and more exhausted than it had been on the 20 September when it had set off north. On October 14 1066 Harold was killed and the Saxons defeated at the Battle of Hastings. Yet, the outcome of the Norman invasion of England might have been very different if the Battle of Stamford Bridge had not taken place.

3

John Paul Jones: An American Hero off Flamborough Head

During the years 2006/7 one of the most exciting underwater searches in modern times is due to take place off the Yorkshire coast. An American-led expedition aims to locate the wreck of one of the USA's very first warships, the *Bonhomme Richard*, which sank somewhere off Flamborough Head in 1779 after an epic battle with the British warship, *Serapis*. The *Bonhomme Richard* was the flagship of the colourful, American naval hero, John Paul Jones. Against great odds, Jones won a momentous victory against the Royal Navy during the American War of Independence.

The arrival in Bridlington of ships from Connecticut's Ocean Technology Foundation, together with US navy vessels, heralded, in June 2006, the start of a six-week, 'high-tech', exploration of the seabed. They will look for signs of the *Bonhomme Richard*, the American warship that sank in the North Sea in 1779. The present-day welcome given to the Americans by the people of Bridlington will be in marked contrast to the situation in September 1779 when the town had been reduced to a state of abject terror by the exploits of Capt. John Paul Jones who was known to be cruising off the Yorkshire coast in search of prey. A large fleet of British coastal vessels had sailed into Bridlington Bay seeking sanctuary from Jones and the harbour was so crowded with ships that many had to be chained together on the outside of the piers. Two companies of the Northumberland Militia who were stationed in the town and local inhabitants who could bear arms were mustered at Bridlington Quay in preparation to repel an expected invasion. With business at a standstill those Bridlington folk who were wealthy enough were making preparations to evacuate their families inland and out of harm's way. Bridlington had every reason to fear an attack since Jones had earlier launched a daring assault on the town of Whitehaven on England's west coast.

In the event Bridlington remained safe from American attack. Instead, on the evening of September 23 1779, local people were to hear gunfire out at sea and those who hastened to the cliffs at Flamborough were able to watch one of the most desperate naval battles in history taking place by moonlight!

The Battle off Flamborough Head was the zenith of Jones's distinguished, but controversial, maritime career. He had been born in 1747 under the name of John Paul at Kirkbean on the shores of Scotland's Solway Firth. Of working class parents he became a seaman's apprentice at the age of thirteen sailing out of the port of Whitehaven. His connection with America was established early for his first voyage took him to Fredericksburg, Virginia where his older brother was living. By the age of seventeen he had joined the slave trade as third mate on the *King George*

Left: Portrait of John Paul Jones painted in around 1890 by George Matthews and based on an earlier picture by Charles Peale (1741-1827).

Opposite: The *Bonhomme Richard*, Jones's flagship, at the battle off Flamborough Head.

of Whitehaven and two years later in 1766 he had become first mate on a slaving vessel called the *Two Friends* carrying slaves from West Africa to Jamaica. Two years later, however, he quit what he later called this 'abominable trade' and by a stroke of good fortune became the captain of another ship sailing to Scotland.

It is a measure of his abilities and determination that Jones rose from ship's boy (at age thirteen) to captain by the age of twenty-one. However, by his twenties he was also showing an unpleasant and violent streak to his character. Jones was a ruthless disciplinarian and as captain of the *John*, operating in the West Indies, was accused by the ship's carpenter of having flogged him excessively with the cat o' nine tails. Worse was to follow. In 1773 while captain of another merchant vessel he quelled what he claimed was a mutiny (in reality, a dispute over wages) by killing one of his crew with a sword. Forced to flee to America he changed his name first to John Jones and later to John Paul Jones. A violent temper was a fault that continued to plague Jones throughout his career and during a critical phase of the Battle off Flamborough Head, for example, he hurled a pistol, in anger, at one of the crew of the *Bonhomme Richard*, knocking him unconscious (see frontispiece).

His arrival in Virginia in 1773 was fortuitous in that his services would soon be needed in the growing disputes between Britain and her American colonies. During 1775 a new naval force to resist the British was being formed and Jones's abilities together with the influence of important patrons meant that he was the first man to be given the rank of 1st Lieutenant in the new Continental Navy (December 22 1775). The American Declaration of Independence followed on the 4 July 1776 and Jones gained useful experience of naval warfare, first aboard the *Alfred* and, from August 1776, as captain of the *Providence*.

By 1777 Jones was advocating a new strategy of fighting Britain at sea. He saw that America's tiny navy was not strong enough to protect its own coasts and said that it should attack the British where they least expected it and where they were most vulnerable. This strategy was to lead to him to Europe where Jones was able to launch a kind of guerrilla warfare against the British in their own home waters with the idea of forcing them to re-assign some of their naval squadrons away from the American coast.

With the French now America's allies, the new strategy began in April 1778 with a month long campaign in the Irish Sea in his ship the *Ranger*. Sailing from the port of Brest he captured or destroyed small British vessels, carried out a hit-and run raid on the town of Whitehaven, launched another in the familiar waters of Kirkudbright Bay in Scotland and captured the 20-gun sloop, HMS *Drake*, off the coast of Northern Ireland. These successes had the desired effect of making the name of John Paul Jones feared throughout Britain although at the time he was reviled as a 'freebooter' and a 'blood-thirsty pirate'.

His victories off Britain's west coast in *Ranger* meant that Jones was given command of a new flotilla of ships. One of these was the *Duc de Duras*, an old merchant vessel given to America by a French shipping magnate, which Jones transformed into a warship with 40 guns and re-named the *Bonhomme Richard*. In addition to this Commodore Jones had at his disposal the *Alliance* a frigate with 36 guns and commanded by a Frenchman, and the *Pallas* a French ship of 32 guns, together with a smaller vessel. On the 14 August 1779 this flotilla of ships set sail on another cruise of the British coast with the aim of destroying or capturing ships involved in the Baltic trade.

On the 23 September 1779 the American fleet of four ships encountered a Baltic convoy off the Yorkshire coast and prepared to intercept it. The forty-one merchant ships were protected by two

British warships: the *Serapis* with fifty guns and the *Countess of Scarborough* with twenty guns. On the face of it the Americans lacked the firepower to deal with such formidable British warships but such was the tenacity of Commodore Jones that he did not consider the possibility of giving up without a fight. Although the main interest in the battle off Flamborough Head centred on the duel between the *Bonhomme Richard*, commanded by Jones himself, and the *Serapis* commanded by Richard Pearson, there was a second battle between the *Pallas* and the *Countess of Scarborough*.

The battle commenced around 7 p.m. under moonlit skies and on a 'millpond' sea with the *Bonhomme Richard* and the *Serapis* firing broadsides at each other. Given the superiority in guns of the *Serapis*, Jones could not hope to win by firepower alone, especially when during a second broadside by the *Bonhomme Richard*, two of his biggest guns exploded killing both officers and men. Jones was forced by circumstances to opt for close-quarters fighting and by skilful seamanship he was able to bring the *Bonhomme Richard* alongside the Serapis by using grappling hooks and lines. There then began a desperate and bloody fight between the crews of the two vessels as a prelude to sending across boarding parties. Even with the two ships locked together the British gunners continued to fire, wreaking havoc with the hull and lower decks of the *Bonhomme Richard*; these were so punched with holes that the sea began to flood in.

The terrors of close-quarter battle between battleships at the time were vividly described by a British prisoner aboard the *Bonhomme Richard*:

> The first impression was of pandemonium let loose. The thunder of the cannon, the pall of thick smoke, the crowds of men naked to the waist rushing hither and thither, their shouting, cursing and screaming, the tops manned with marksmen, the groans of the wounded as they were carried below decks strewn with wreckage and red with blood- a spectacle frightful and fiendish.

As the three and a half hour battle reached its bloody climax the damage done to the *Bonhomme Richard* was such that the ship was sinking. The master-at-arms, despite his captain's orders to the

Right: A painting by Dean Mosher depicting the damage suffered by the American ship *Bonhomme Richard* by HMS *Serapis* during the battle. (courtsey Dean Mosher)

Opposite: The coastline at Flamborough Head from where local people watched the battle between the Americans and the Royal Navy under moonlit skies.

contrary, released one hundred British prisoners and told them to man the pumps to stop the ship from going under. As Jones directed grape-shot from his few remaining guns and musket fire onto the decks of the *Serapis*, fire broke out on both ships; aloft in the sails and below decks. With over half the American crew dead or wounded the situation looked hopeless for Jones but he fought on stubbornly and when asked if he wished to surrender by Pearson defiantly declared, 'I have not yet begun to fight'.

It was then that fate intervened. According to Jones's own journal one of his crew, William Hamilton, high up on the main yard of the *Bonhomme Richard*, began throwing grenades down onto the deck of the *Serapis* below. It seems that one of these fell into an open hatchway and exploded near ammunition stacked close to the port side guns. This created a flash fire that detonated yet more explosives killing twenty British crewmen and injuring many more. With this disaster the guns of the *Serapis* fell silent and when the *Alliance* too joined in the battle against her Captain Pearson decided to surrender his ship to Jones. The *Countess of Scarborough* had surrendered earlier to the *Pallas* after a two-hour battle.

Despite the unfavourable odds the Americans had prevailed against the superior British ships pitted against them. However, attempts to stop the *Bonhomme Richard* from sinking proved fruitless and she sank under the waters of the North Sea on the 25 September taking with her Jones's clothes, books and personal possessions. Now in control of the *Serapis* Jones sailed for Texel in Holland and a hero's welcome. The public adulation and honours he received in France from King Louis XVI went to his head and what many considered to be his insufferable flair for self-promotion served to irritate friends and fellow officers alike.

Despite his often tactlessness and selfish behaviour there is no doubt he showed courage and ability as a naval tactician and had the power to inspire a nation. By his victory over the British off Flamborough Head on 23 September 1779 Jones became a hero of the American Revolution and is considered by many to be the 'Father of the American Navy'.

4

The Riding At War: When the Blitz Came to Beverley

In comparison to the city of Hull the town of Beverley was largely untouched by the bombs of the Luftwaffe . However, on one fateful day in August 1942 that situation was to dramatically change.

It was widely believed that when the Second World War began, in September 1939, all of Britain's major towns and cities would be immediately subjected to a massive bombardment by the German air force. In fact that bombardment was postponed until after the fall of France in June 1940. The first serious raids against Hull and other major cities began in August 1940 and reached a new intensity during the early months of 1941. The city of Hull was an easy target for even inexperienced Luftwaffe crews to find as it lay at the junction of the Rivers Hull and Humber. The air raids of the 7-9 May 1941 were particularly devastating with huge quantities of high explosive and incendiary bombs destroying large parts of Hull's city centre. Casualties for these nights were 450 killed and 350 seriously injured.

In comparison to the blitz on Hull the villages and towns of the East Riding remained largely unscathed although there was a taste of the aerial assault to come in October 1940 when an enemy aircraft passing over Leven and Beverley machine gunned property and people. In North Bar Street, Beverley, three people waiting at a bus stop at around 6 p.m. were injured and there was damage to property in King's Square, Walkergate and the Causeway caused by machine gun bullets. In Register Square, Pottage's shop was set alight by incendiary bullets.

When the bombing began in earnest many of the bombs that fell on Beverley were destined for Hull but due to poor visibility, or inexperienced bomber crews, ended up elsewhere. The records of the Beverley Air Raid Control Centre held by the East Riding Archives Service show, in horrifying detail, where these bombs fell. On the night of the 18/19 March 1941 the Luftwaffe's primary target was Hull with 464 long range and 19 light bombers assigned to the operation. However, whether by miscalculation or design, the Victoria Barracks in Beverley (where Morrison's Store now stands) was hit by two parachute mines at 1.05 a.m. As well as extensive damage, three military personnel were killed and fifteen other casualties were removed to the Beverley Base Hospital (now the Westwood Hospital). That same night one high explosive bomb was dropped on Model Farm on Hull Bridge Road, and two on Cherry Tree Lane, Beverley. Although there was damage to farm buildings and other property in neither case were there casualties.

As well as the Victoria Barracks another military target close to Beverley was Leconfield Aerodrome. Opened on December 3 1936 this RAF station occupied 1,000 acres at the south

The public was warned of the danger of gas attacks.

east end of the village. Originally used as a bomber base, by 1939-1940 both Spitfires and Hurricanes were stationed there. On the 13 July 1940 Number 302 squadron of the Polish Air Force was formed at Leconfield and began training with Hurricane fighters.

Like other RAF stations Leconfield became a target for the Luftwaffe. On the 27 October 1940 five high-explosive bombs were dropped on the base. Although it was reported that damage was 'negligible', there was one casualty: a Polish airman of 302 Squadron. The Germans made a more determined effort in May 1941 when 23 high-explosive and 250 incendiary bombs missed their intended target and fell on Leconfield Grange Farm instead.

The heavy raids of May 1941 against Hull also brought death and destruction on a smaller scale to the East Riding. On the 9 May a parachute mine exploded in Ferry Lane Woodmansey killing Harry Sinyard, aged 36, of Wood Villa and seriously injuring his wife, together with three others. Ambulances and first-aid parties from Beverley and Walkington were dispatched to Woodmansey to deal with the injured. A total of six houses were damaged in this incident and Ferry Lane was blocked for a time.

As in the recent war against Iraq the authorities were alarmed that the enemy might be prepared to use poison gas attacks. The civilian population were told to be vigilant and exhorted

Once used solely by the RAF, Leconfield Aerodrome is now Normandy Barracks and home to the joint armed services school of transport.

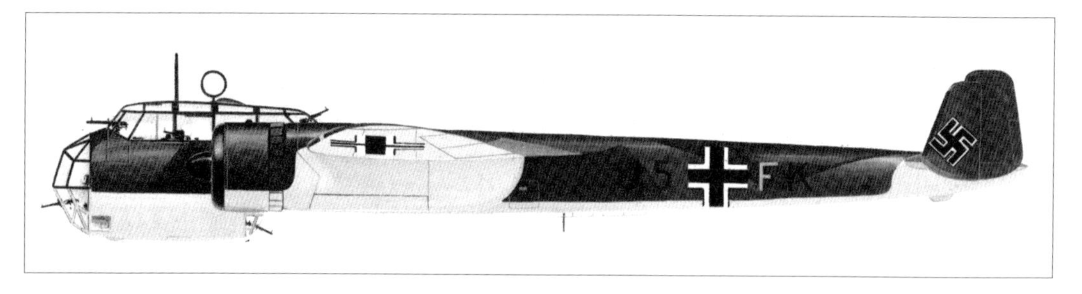

Beverley's most serious air raid of the war took place on Bank Holiday Monday, 3 August 1942, when a single Dornier bomber passed over the town.

to carry gas masks at all times. Any likely gas bombs were investigated thoroughly. Thus on the 17 May 1941 a bomb fell on the Etton to South Dalton road and scattered about ten gallons of a suspicious liquid. A report on the incident was sent to the 'Senior Gas Advisor', Professor Challenger of Leeds University although the suspicious liquid turned out to be oil from an incendiary bomb.

It is clear too that Britain's armed forces had made their own preparations for gas warfare for on the 2 April 1942 four boys aged between 11 and 13 broke into a military gas compound in Figham, Beverley. Three of the boys were detained in the Beverley Base Hospital suffering from mustard gas burns while their clothing was collected by the Beverley Borough authorities for 'decontamination'.

Beverley's most serious air raid of the war took place on Bank Holiday Monday, 3 August 1942, when a single Dornier bomber passed over the town. Beverley had its share of military targets like the Armstrong's factory in Eastgate which made tracer-shell casings for the Royal Navy. However, in this case the primary target seems to have been Hodgson's Tannery in Flemingate although with the crude bomb-aiming capabilities of the time there were likely to be other casualties. A detailed report in the East Riding Archive shows that a total of four 500kg high explosive bombs hit the area at about 5.55 p.m. and that one of these failed to explode.

The first bomb caused extensive damage to the tannery, the second landed in Flemingate in front of Brentwood Villas and a third exploded behind Flemingate Methodist chapel. The Flemingate bombs led directly to three deaths. No. 4 Brentwood Villas was the home of Ralph Snowden and his wife Francis. One of the bombs exploding directly in front of it demolished the front wall of the house and buried the occupants under rubble. Francis Snowden was killed outright by the blast and her husband, who already had heart problems, was to die four months later. Another fatality was Mr Charles Cross of Sparkmill Cottages who was feeding his rabbits when the third bomb ricocheted from the tannery over the houses in Flemingate and exploded behind the Methodist chapel. The third death was Lieutenant Stanley Lawrence, caught in the second explosion as he cycled along Flemingate past Brentwood Villas. There were also some narrow escapes. Mrs Blanche Kirkby of No. 1 Sparkmill Terrace had been outside only moments before the third bomb exploded. She was rescued and taken to hospital with head injuries. Another resident, outside feeding his pigs, escaped with nothing more than a black eye. In total, there were fifteen other casualties ranging from lacerations to shock.

Damage to property was considerable with twelve houses being made uninhabitable and about fifty others suffering broken windows, collapsed ceilings, smashed roof tiles and so on. The Civil Defence services were quickly deployed to rescue those trapped in the wreckage of their homes, to clear Flemingate of debris and to ferry the injured to the Beverley Base Hospital. In a spirit of cooperation and solidarity, arrangements were quickly made with the City Engineer's Department in Hull to dispatch bricklayers, joiners, plumbers and other workers to Flemingate to carry out repairs to bomb-damaged property.

Many more lives might have been lost that day had it not been for the element of chance. Beverley's most serious raid of the war took place on a Bank Holiday in late afternoon when several Flemingate residents had taken their children to the cinema. Arthur Lucan was appearing in an 'Old Mother Riley' film then showing at the Marble Arch cinema in Butcher Row (where Somerfield now stands). It was said at the time that many owed their very lives to Old Mother Riley!

5

Rough and Tumble: Beverley's Turbulent Elections of the Past

In twenty-first-century elections the power of television is used by political parties to influence public opinion and win electoral support. It is interesting to look at a time when candidates used far different methods to secure votes.

Anyone who votes in parliamentary or local elections today will recognise the safeguards built into Britain's modern voting system to ensure fairness and prevent cheating. Although politicians may try to discover the intentions of the voters through opinion polls and canvassing the secret ballot ensures complete privacy at the polling station. Less than one hundred and fifty years ago voting in secret did not exist and it was commonplace for election results to be influenced by bribery, threats and sharp practice of all kinds.

Beverley has been sending people to Parliament since Medieval times and the right to choose two Members of Parliament was confirmed by a charter of Elizabeth I in 1573. However this *choosing* fell far short of modern standards. In the first place relatively few adults had the right to vote; in Beverley, before 1832, the right to vote belonged exclusively to a select group of men called the freemen of the borough. It was not necessary, either, for these freemen to be resident in Beverley. In the 1818 parliamentary election about 38% of the voters lived outside the town and in some cases at a great distance away. Since voting was not in secret we can see how the freemen cast their votes by looking at the poll books which were published after the election.

Of course, there was only a need for an election if there were more than two candidates. Many of the freemen of Beverley were anxious to ensure that there was a 'Third Man' at election time, simply to make the other candidates more generous with their money. Paying money to the electors, although illegal, was a common practice during the eighteenth and nineteenth centuries and most candidates got away with it. However, in 1728 it was proved that a winning candidate, Ellerker Bradshaw, had used bribery on a huge scale paying each voter £3 3s 0d and as a result he forfeited his seat in Parliament. Although nothing could be proved against Bradshaw himself his election agents were found guilty of 'notorious and scandalous bribery and corruption' and were imprisoned in Newgate gaol.

Any person hoping to become an MP for Beverley had to have either a large fortune or a wealthy patron. Large sums were spent by candidates on the travelling and living expenses of voters who lived outside the town. In 1826, for example, the expenses of over 200 of these 'out voters' cost John Stewart more than £600 and in the case of several London voters £6 was allowed to each of them in travelling expenses. On election day itself the voters expected

A Copy of the Poll.

VOTERS' NAMES.

☞ The Persons whose places of Residence are not mentioned, live in or near Beverley.

A.	CANDIDATES.		
	BUR.	SYK.	CUR.
Abbott John, innkeeper	306		176
Abbott William, cordwainer	281		155
Abbott Thomas, ditto	599		381
Abbott Jonathan, mariner	790		490
Acklam William Etty, currier, *Hull*	196		
Acklam George, cordwainer, *Seaton*	94	44	
Acklam James Leighton, East India House Commodore, *London*	755	498	
Acklam Stephen, gentleman		378	
Acklam James, cordwainer, *Fridaythorpe*	943	638	
Ackrill William, innkeeper	433		267
Ackrill Esau, gun-maker	471		296
Adamson William, potter	75		
Adamson Richard, breeches-maker		412	
Adamson Thomas, bleacher, *Harrogate*	95		61
Akester William, cordwainer	378		231
Akester William, jun. ditto	260		145
Akester Robert, shipwright, *Hull*	217	113	
Alcroft Joseph, blacksmith, *ditto*	578		368

In the days before secret ballots the votes of each elector were recorded in a poll book like this one for 1830. It was thus easy to see after the election how electors had cast their votes. Bribery and intimidation of voters was widespread.

the candidates to provide food and drink. Innkeepers played an important part in the elections of this period and their premises often became the headquarters of particular candidates. The Beverley Arms, for example, was the centre of a number of campaigns including that of Henry Burton in 1830. The election accounts of Burton make fascinating reading and show a mass of payments to people like musicians (£287), flag carriers (£94) and 'men for assisting the infirm to the poll' (£2). Of course it is open to question how far these expenses were really disguised bribes. Whatever the truth, Burton's accounts show that he spent £3,200 on his election in 1830, a huge sum by nineteenth-century standards. The cost of elections could also lead to financial ruin; John Wharton, MP for Beverley 1790-96 and 1802-26, was so deeply in debt at the time of his defeat in 1826 that he spent the last fourteen years of his life in prison.

The expenses of the successful candidates did not end on election day. To maintain their popularity between elections Beverley's MPs were expected to contribute to worthy local causes like payments in support of Beverley Races and the Charity School. In 1708 the sitting MPs, Sir Michael Wharton and Sir Charles Hotham, were asked to contribute towards the cost of a new Market Cross in Beverley.

Beverley elections of the past were frequently marked by acts of violence, usually caused by the drunken excesses of the mob in an age when policing was inadequate. Fuelled by drink the situation could rapidly get out of hand. In 1722 the behaviour of Michel Newton's mob became

The Beverley Arms was the centre of a number of political campaigns including that of Henry Burton in 1830.

increasingly violent and they attacked the son of Sir Charles Hotham, a rival candidate. To save his life Sir Charles drew his sword and threatened to kill Newton unless he stopped his mob.

During the by-election of 1799 it seems the mob supported John Wharton rather than his rival, John Morritt. During a canvass of the town Morritt and his supporters were parading with a flag and music when they were set upon by Wharton's followers who were armed with large sticks. A letter of the time records how Wharton's men:

> … gave no quarter either to Mr Morritt nor his flag, for it was tore in pieces in a moment and several of the men much bruised, and Mr Morritt was obliged to take refuge in a poor person's house until the mob dispersed …

Despite his narrow escape from violence John Morritt went on to win the election by 512 votes to Wharton's 369!

Although eighteenth-century electioneering could be a rough business, the candidates themselves usually treated each other with courtesy. However, in 1806 John Wharton took exception to some remarks made by his rival, Napier Christie Burton and challenged him to a duel. After a case of pistols had been fired honour was satisfied!

Despite parliamentary reform in the nineteenth century which, among other things, extended the vote to more Beverley householders, many of the worst features of the old system continued.

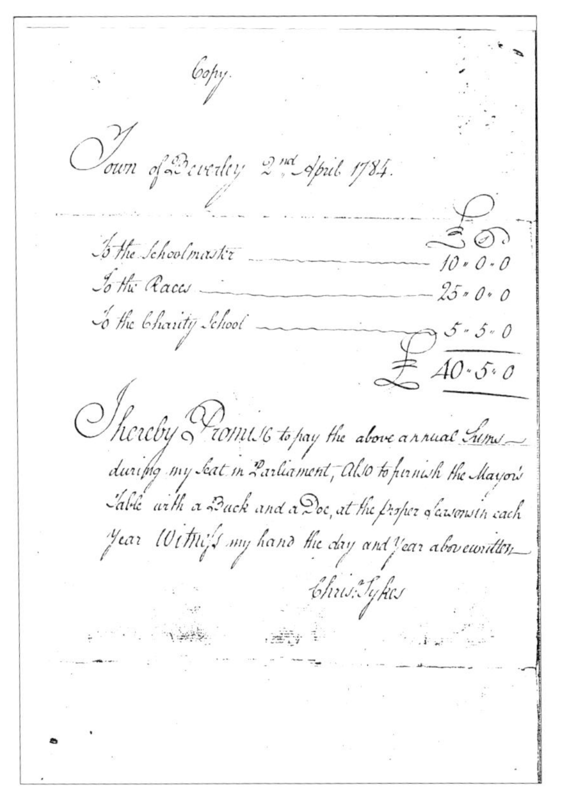

Copy.

Town of Beverley 2nd April 1784.

	£ s d
To the Schoolmaster	10 . 0 . 0
To the Races	25 . 0 . 0
To the Charity School	5 . 5 . 0
	£ 40 . 5 . 0

I hereby Promise to pay the above annual Sums during my Seat in Parliament, also to furnish the Mayor's Table with a Buck and a Doe, at the Proper season each Year Witness my hand the day and Year abovewritten

Chris: Sykes

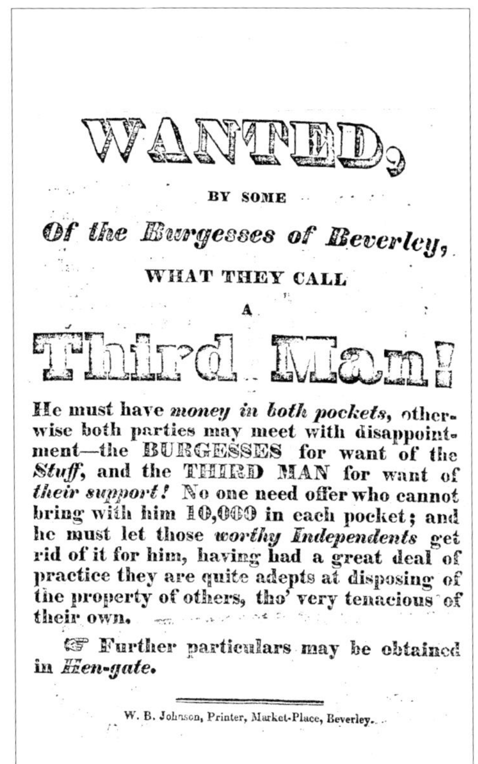

WANTED,

BY SOME

Of the Burgesses of Beverley,

WHAT THEY CALL

A

Third Man!

He must have *money in both pockets,* otherwise both parties may meet with disappointment—the BURGESSES for want of the *Stuff,* and the THIRD MAN for want of *their support!* No one need offer who cannot bring with him 10,000 in each pocket; and he must let those *worthy Independents* get rid of it for him, having had a great deal of practice they are quite adepts at disposing of the property of others, tho' very tenacious of their own.

☞ Further particulars may be obtained in *Hen-gate.*

W. B. Johnson, Printer, Market-Place, Beverley.

Above left: The promises made by Christopher Sykes MP in 1784. The generosity of Beverley MPs did not end on election day. They were also expected to contribute to 'worthy causes' like Beverley Races.

Above right: A sarcastic poster from the early nineteenth century making fun of the eagerness of Beverley electors for there to be a 'third man' at election times.

The town became so notorious throughout Britain for its bribery, corruption and electoral abuses that in 1869 a Royal Commission was set up to investigate. The Commissioners heard that more than a third of the electorate had been bribed during the election of 1868. During this contest the novelist Anthony Trollope had stood as one of the Liberal candidates but, presumably because he did not pay bribes, failed to be elected. Disgusted by the corruption of the town Trollope used it as the setting for his novel *Ralph the Heir.*

As a result of the Royal Commission's findings Beverley lost its right to have its own MPs in 1870; the unsavoury evidence collected also helped to persuade Parliament to bring in the secret ballot in 1872. There is no doubt that the rough and tumble of Beverley's parliamentary elections offended the Victorians' sense of morality and helped to usher in laws to stem the worst features of the old system.

6

Hull's Focus of Discontent: James Acland, Nineteenth-Century Agitator

Like many places in England the town of Hull, in the early nineteenth century, was governed by an undemocratic and corrupt corporation. Yet changing the way towns were run, in the decades following the French Revolution, was almost as dangerous as bringing pressure to change the way Parliament was elected. Even so there were individuals who were prepared to risk persecution and imprisonment to right wrongs and campaign for reform. One such agitator was James Acland who in 1831 arrived in Hull to begin his campaign against Hull Corporation.

James Acland, the son of a butcher, was born in London in 1799. When he was only twelve years old his father became bankrupt and this may have contributed to Acland's ambition, as he put it, to be 'self-reliant'. From the evidence it seems Acland was a volatile character with a brisk self-confidence and a natural gift for oratory. These attributes probably made him difficult to live with and, by his own admission, family disagreements persuaded him to leave home and seek his fortune. By the age of sixteen he was living in Bristol and soon became a controversial figure with his outspoken views on Bristol Corporation and by championing the cause of people unjustly convicted by the Corporation in its role as magistrate. In May 1827 Acland, in search of a reliable income to support his family, started a newspaper called *The Bristolian*. A radical by nature Acland used his newspaper to accuse the magistrates of incompetence and he was soon in trouble; during June and July 1827 he was ejected from the courts on numerous occasions. Embarrassed by Acland's newspaper campaigns Bristol Corporation brought actions against him for libel and he was sentenced to a term of imprisonment.

In 1831 Acland moved to Hull and immediately launched into new attacks against those who wielded political power locally. In the style of his *Bristolian* newspaper he started the *Hull Portfolio*. This had the clear intention of drawing attention to the incompetence of local magistrates and bringing an end to corporation rule. One of his early campaigns was about Hull's Market Place which he criticised as being far too small. Acland suggested that the congestion around the market arose from the Corporation's policy of allowing vendors to set out their goods in surrounding side streets. Acland's scathing style of writing soon attracted a large readership to the *Hull Portfolio* for as George Codd, Hull's town clerk put it, 'abuse and reformation of the Corporation were a passport to popularity'.

One of Acland's most famous campaigns against Hull Corporation was on the issue of their ferry monopoly across the River Humber to Barton. Acland accused the Corporation of using their position as sole provider to charge exorbitant fares and claimed, by reference to old

James Acland, radical agitator.

charters, that this was illegal. To challenge the monopoly of the legal ferry Acland, in September 1831, established a rival ferryboat called the *Public Opinion*. In celebration of his defiance he had Hull's coat of arms painted upside down on the boat's paddle boxes. The fare on Acland's boat was half that charged by the legal ferry and people flocked to use it. Later in the year, after a collision between the two ferries, the Corporation impounded Acland's boat and this led to ugly scenes at the Hull jetty when, in retaliation, thousands of people tried to prevent the official boat from berthing.

While Acland was engaged in breaking the Corporation's Humber ferry monopoly he was also drawing attention to its market tolls. He claimed that the tolls were illegal and in typical Acland style announced his intention of setting up a stall in the market place and not paying the toll. On November 1 1831, watched by a large crowd, he set up a stall at the foot of King William's statue and flew flags marked Free Trade and No Tolls. He then began selling ginger bread figures of the mayor and aldermen while calling on other stall-holders to follow his example by refusing to pay the tolls. In the following ten months the Corporation was to lose about £700 in market tolls before they were able to prove, in a test case, that they were entitled to collect them.

THE

Hull Portfolio;

OR

MEMOIRS AND CORRESPONDENCE OF

JAMES ACLAND

ITS PROPRIETOR AND EDITOR.

"BONIS NOCET QUISQUIS PEPERCERIT MALIS."—*Cicero.*
He injures the good who spares the bad.

VOLUME THE FIRST,

Commencing Aug. 20th, and terminating. Dec. 31st, 1831.

JAMES ACLAND,
PRINTER AND PUBLISHER,
Queen-Street,
HULL.

Left: The title page of James Acland's *Hull Portfolio* newspaper. Note he shows contempt for Hull Corporation by putting Hull's 'three crowns' upside down!

Below: Acland's protest against the market tolls from a contemporary drawing.

This SKETCH of the FIRST ATTEMPT to ABOLISH the MARKET TOLLS of KINGSTON upon HULL. 1st Novr 1831
is Respectfully Dedicated to the Reformers of Hull, by their faithful Servant
James Acland

There is no doubt that Acland's activities cost the corporation dear for during his stay in Hull they spent over £4,000 in legal actions against him.

It is clear that Acland's activities in Hull brought the town to a fever-pitch of excitement and that violence threatened to overwhelm the authorities on numerous occasions. Yet, the evidence shows that Acland did not abuse his power by encouraging his supporters to commit riots. In fact he tried to restrain them from violent acts as in September 1832 when during an unsuccessful attempt to get himself elected as town chamberlain, scuffles broke out and troops were summoned. From the window of a house overlooking the confrontation Acland appealed to both sides for calm and defused a volatile situation.

As in Bristol previously, Acland's campaigns did not go unchallenged by the people he attacked and in March 1832 he faced trial for infringing the Corporation's ferry monopoly. Although he was found guilty the judge only awarded damages of one farthing to the Corporation! His enemies also sought to silence him through libel actions for his words in the *Hull Portfolio* when he had accused members of the corporation of dishonesty, vice and ignorance. Once again he was found guilty and served eighteen months in prison at Bury St Edmunds. His wife too suffered for she was imprisoned in the Beverley House of Correction for trying to publish the *Hull Portfolio* in his absence.

While Acland languished in prison his cherished hope of local government reform was set in motion when commissioners visited Hull as part of their national enquiry into municipal corporations. From his prison cell Acland sent them information and many of the criticisms he had made of the Corporation were substantiated in their findings about Hull. The national report of the commissioners led to a radical overhaul of local government under the Municipal Corporations Act, reforms that Acland had long advocated. After the passing of the Municipal Corporations Act in 1835 not a single member of the old corporation was re-elected. Town councillors now had to seek re-election at regular intervals.

The end of Acland's tormentors, however, lay in the future, for on his release from Bury St Edmunds gaol (summer 1834) the old unreformed Hull Corporation still held sway. Acland did not stay out of trouble for long. He returned to Hull and from his home in Queen Street, which he called the 'Anti-Corporate Castle', he sold 'anti-corporate tea', 'public opinion coffee' and 'radical tobacco'. He also launched several short-lived publications to replace the *Hull Portfolio* including one called *The Libel*! At a time of the taxation of knowledge Acland was soon sentenced to further imprisonment (this time in Hull) for selling unstamped newspapers. Even from his prison cell Acland continued to support radical causes by editing a new publication called, appropriately, *Prison Proverbs*.

Acland's career as a radical agitator and mob leader, therefore, was not without its hardships and dangers and it is a mark of the man that he was prepared, in his quest for natural justice, to suffer numerous spells in prison for the causes he believed in. In his seventies he was to write of the years spent in Tory prisons for, 'having dared to write and publish severe truths of very bad Tory functionaries when truth was held by servile judges to be libellous....'

Yet, Acland considered the sacrifice to have been worth it for, as he said, his campaigns had assisted his fellow creatures through the 'repeal of bad laws' and establishing a free press where 'truth is no longer a libel'.

7

A Great Survivor: The Rise and Rise of Bartoline

In May 2003 a devastating fire took hold of the Barmston Close premises of one of Beverley's oldest family companies, Bartoline. Today, an up-to-date factory complex has risen from the ashes of the old.

In a fast-moving world successful industrial enterprises are usually those which can readily adapt to changing market conditions. The success of Bartoline of Beverley seems to owe much to the ability of that company to keep abreast of modern trends and to change its products accordingly.

The company's origins can be traced back to 1876 when Richard Barton, the son of an Easingwold school teacher, began a coal exporting business in Hull. The enterprise developed by trading in ship stores and lubricating oil and, in 1912, became known as Bartoline (Hull) Ltd. The offices of the company moved to Myton Place while the main Bartoline factory was at Fawcitt Street. The manufacturing side, at this early stage in the company's development, was hardly the most environmentally friendly since the products made included lubricating oils for industry, greases, and bituminous paint and both the factory and its employees were perpetually covered in grime!

At a time when businesses tended to be small family run affairs the survival of the new company owed much to the determination and ability of Richard Barton's offspring. In 1903 a son from his first marriage, Wilfred Barton, a solicitor, had injected much-needed capital into the firm. After the death of Richard Barton in 1927 a son from his second marriage, John Barton, became managing director of the company and this was to herald changes to the product range of the company that would be lucrative. With the rise of private motoring in the twenties and thirties more emphasis was now given to motor oils. Under John Barton's leadership the number of specialist engine lubricants increased to ten and a Bartoline price list from 1931 shows their most popular brand, XL High Speed Motor Oil, was being sold for 4 shillings a gallon. Among the slogans devised by the company in the thirties to market their motor oils were:

Don't change gear - change to Bartoline.

Bartoline - the best in the long run.

The changes brought in by John Barton helped to make the company more profitable and put it on a firm financial footing for the first time in its history. An astute businessman, he realised

Above: By the 1920s Bartoline Motor Oil was being sold in tin containers. (courtesy Bartoline Ltd)

Left: The origins of Bartoline Ltd can be traced back to 1876 when Richard Barton, the son of an Easingwold school teacher, began a coal exporting business in Hull. (courtesy Bartoline Ltd

that change and adaptability were the keys to success and as competition in lubricating oils increased so other products, like protective paints, came to the fore.

When the Second World War began in 1939 Bartoline, with its range of highly inflammable products and raw materials, was in a very vulnerable position in a major target city like Hull. Yet despite the heavy raids on the city in May 1941, the factory escaped largely unscathed. In 1940 John Barton had transferred the company's offices from Myton Place to Cottingham and it remained there until after the war ended.

The uncertainties of the war years were followed by the uncertainties of the post-war period. In 1945 the Lutyens and Abercrombie Plan on the future of Hull was published and this included far-reaching proposals for the re-siting of the town's industry. However, the austerity of the post-war years delayed the City Council's plans to re-develop the city centre and postponed for almost twenty years, Bartoline's plans to move elsewhere. Compensation of £12,500 for their existing premises largely financed a move, in 1964, to Air Street, off Bankside. Even this transfer was relatively short-lived; expansion was impossible at Air Street and the company was soon looking for new premises.

At the same time as Bartoline moved to Air Street in Hull, Beverley Borough Council were seeking to foster new light industries in the town by creating the Swinemoor Lane Industrial Estate. This began to attract a variety of firms and in 1968 Bartoline was able to secure a greenfield site at Barmston Close.

The post-war changes of location were matched by developments to its product range including multi-grade motor oils, adhesives, rust removers and liquid detergents. The 1960s were the boom years of the British car industry and a large market for Bartoline chassis black paint

The offices of Bartoline at Myton Place, Hull. (drawing by F.S. Smith, courtesy Hull Local Studies Library)

and turps subsititute was created in the West Midlands by a host of famous motoring names (now sadly extinct) including Riley, Hillman, Wolsey and Austin. There were additions to the Bartoline family of lubricants too including a confectionary oil to stop sweets sticking during manufacture. This Bartoline 'white slab oil' was sold nationally to a range of customers from Scarborough rock makers to household confectionary names like Rowntrees and Cadburys.

A major factor in the Bartoline success story was the export trade, so much so that by 1977 the company was exporting 75% of its products. Much of this trade was to the Middle East and the slogan 'selling oil to the Arabs' reflected Bartoline's long experience as oil-refiners. The export achievements of the company were marked by a visit to the Beverley factory by the Duke of Kent in November 1977. Further recognition for their export achievements came in 1980 with an invitation to a Buckingham Palace garden party for Richard Barton and his wife Susan.

Richard Barton had begun working for the company at the war time Cottingham office when aged sixteen and, after National Service, re-joined the company in 1949. Within twelve years he had risen to the post of managing director and under his watchful eye the company, in the 1980s, developed more products for the expanding DIY sector. The staple Bartoline products of creosote, turpentine substitute and motor oil were now attractively packaged into small retail containers while new markets for these (together with innovative leisure products like barbecue lighting fluid) were created among the multiple DIY and supermarket chains across the length and breadth of the country.

The growth of Bartoline's product range and its customer base both in the United Kingdom and overseas resulted, by 1997, in a record turnover of £7 million. By now under the control of a fourth generation member of the family, Simon Barton, this expansion seemed set to continue into the twenty-first century. No-one could have foreseen how the future of the company would be put at risk by the dramatic events of Friday May 23 2003. Some time after 9 a.m. the Bartoline site in Barmston Close was rocked by explosions and engulfed by a fire which destroyed everything in its path. Despite the arrival of thirty-one fire appliances from all over Yorkshire and Lincolnshire there was little they could do to halt the inferno, fuelled by the highly inflammable materials used in the making of solvents, wood preservatives, oils and lubricants. By the evening of May 23, with the Bartoline site in ruins, it seemed that the future of this long established company hung in the balance.

Yet as with previous crises in the firm's long history, Bartoline has shown a remarkable ability to bounce back in the face of adversity. A company which survived the depression of the 1930s, the Hull Blitz of 1941 and the oil crisis and industrial unrest of the 1970s has been able to demonstrate the same resilience in coping with the 2003 disaster. This is despite being handed a bill of £500,000 for an environmental clean-up in the aftermath of the fire.

Supported by the East Riding County Council, temporary premises were secured to re-start production while ambitious plans were set in motion to rebuild. A year on from the inferno of May 2003 a new start-of the-art factory development costing £5 million has begun to rise from the ashes of the old, safeguarding eighty existing jobs and perhaps creating many more.

The new Bartoline factory, equipped with the very latest safety devices to prevent a repeat of one of East Yorkshire's most serious fires of recent times, is now in operation. Its completion has symbolised the triumph of a great survivor in the world of East Yorkshire business and heralds a new chapter in the history of a vibrant enterprise run by four generations of the same family.

The day after the spectacular fire at Bartoline on 23 May 2003.

8

A Great Yorkshire Aircraft Pioneer: Robert Blackburn

The West Yorkshire city of Leeds, the East Yorkshire settlement of Brough and the North Yorkshire town of Filey might not appear to have much in common. However all were to bear witness to the exploits of Robert Blackburn, a Leeds-based engineer and aeronautical pioneer.

The ups and downs of BAE Systems at Brough, in recent times, is a clear reminder of the vital importance of manufacturing jobs to Britain's economy. The continuing existence there of the BAE factory is also testament to the vision, energy and skill of a remarkable Yorkshire engineer and entrepreneur, Robert Blackburn.

He was born on 26 March 1885, the son of George Blackburn the works manager of a Leeds engineering company. Robert's early promise as a school boy was fulfilled when he graduated from Leeds University with an honours degree in engineering. Further study in France brought the twenty-two year old into contact with that country's fledgling aviation industry; his weekends were spent at Le Mans watching Wilbur Wright fly his pioneering biplane. These early experiences fired Blackburn's imagination to the extent that while still in France he completed designs for his first monoplane. Determined to show that his ambition to be an aeroplane designer was no mere flight of fancy he returned to Leeds and persuaded his reluctant father to back his plans for building planes.

Blackburn's first monoplane proved to be a failure when he tried to fly it from a beach in north-east England during 1909/1910. Using a wicker chair from his father's garden as his pilot's seat he made several attempts to lift the under-powered plane from the sands between Marske and Saltburn. Although the plane made a few ungainly hops from the beach even Robert Blackburn later referred to these attempts as 'sand scratching'. His experiments came to an abrupt end in May 1910 when, in attempting a turn, he wrecked his plane.

Blackburn's determination to succeed in the new science of aeronautics, however, was soon shown by designs for a much better plane constructed during 1910–1911. In order to try out the new monoplane he transported it to the Yorkshire coast where the long, firm sands of Filey Bay were ideal for taking off and landing. Blackburn was able to rent a hanger at the Filey aerodrome (opened in July 1910) and an adjoining bungalow for a weekly rent of 10 shillings each. From the hanger at the top of the cliffs planes were winched down a concrete slipway onto the beach below to be tested. Although he had attempted to pilot the first monoplane himself Blackburn now left the flying to others and concentrated on the construction side of the business in Leeds. A pilot called Benfield Hucks took to the air in Blackburn's second monoplane at Filey

Robert Blackburn's career had begun with designs inspired by the Wright Brothers and French aviation pioneers and ended with jet aircraft like the Buccaneer, at the cutting edge of innovation. (courtesy British Aerospace Heritage Centre, Brough, East Yorkshire)

on the 8 March 1911 and promptly crashed it from a height of 30ft while trying to make a turn. However, the machine was repaired and became one of the instructional aircraft which Blackburn used to start a flying school at Filey. This prospered, for a short time at least, under instructors like Hucks who despite his initial crash became a skilled pilot able to stay in the air for three hours at a time The Filey sands were also used to test Blackburn's new design: a two-seater monoplane called the Mercury. This was exhibited at the Olympia Aero show in London in 1911 and several versions of the Mercury were built over the next two years. However, there were danger's involved in handling these early aircraft, when flying was still in its infancy. This was well illustrated when the second of Blackburn's test pilots and instructors, Hubert Oxley, took to the skies above Filey beach in December 1911. Flying the fourth Mercury monoplane to bear that name he carried a student pilot called Robert Weiss, the son of a well-to-do wool trading family from Dewsbury. Whether by accident or pilot error the machine went into a steep dive and crashed onto the beach. Oxley was thrown from the plane and died of a broken neck while Weiss died less than an hour later from multiple injuries.

Although the Filey Flying School was relatively short lived, moving to Hendon in September 1912, Blackburn's business in Leeds prospered with orders from the Royal Flying Corps and the Royal Naval Air Service. The outbreak of the First World War in August 1914 and the consequent government orders for over 100 biplanes meant that the Blackburn Aeroplane and Motor Company Co Ltd (as it was now known) was able to expand rapidly. The company took possession of a disused roller-skating rink in Roundhay Road, Leeds and this became the centre of the Blackburn aircraft building operation. A decision was also made to build a machine shop at the new factory to turn out the small standard parts needed by aircraft manufacturers (nuts, bolts and standard fittings). This was highly successful and helped keep the company in business in the lean years following the end of the war in 1918.

By 1914 Robert Blackburn had developed an interest in aeroplanes which could take off and land on water and a Type L seaplane was the first plane to be built at his new factory. To provide for the seaplane side of the business one of his staff, Mark Swann, was

Robert Blackburn's first attempt to get his plane off the beach on the North-East coast in 1909 was later referred to by him as 'sand scratching'. (courtesy British Aerospace Heritage Centre, Brough, East Yorkshire)

A watercolour by John Ridyard based on a photographic postcard, 1911. Many of Blackburn's early designs were tested over the beach at Filey.

dispatched, in 1916, to find a suitable base as a seaplane testing faculty. Swann examined several sites but recommended the village of Brough, on the north bank of the Humber, as the best one available. Here, adjacent to the Hull-Leeds railway line there was land available to build an aerodrome and access to the Humber for launching marine aircraft. Brough lay at a bend in the river which, in theory, gave it the advantage that seaplanes and flying boats could take off in any wind direction or state of the tide. However, in the light of experience, the base was not as ideal as had been hoped; the Humber tides restricted the times of day when flying boats could be tested while the Humber's own brand of sea-mist known as a fret could make landings at the Brough aerodrome impossible. Commercial decisions, it seems, are sometimes made without access to all the facts!

While, Brough was meant to be, initially, a seaplane testing base between 1928 and 1932 much of the work of the Blackburn Aeroplane Company was transferred there from Leeds. This was to cause acute problems for the 1,000 Leeds employees who were forced to commute there daily by train until they could re-locate to homes which were closer. Members of the Blackburn family themselves moved from the West Riding to the village to be closer to the new centre of operations. The focus on Brough led to its expansion especially during the rearmament years of the 1930s. By now Blackburns were well established as specialists in naval aircraft construction and production of aircraft like the Swift, the Shark and the Skua kept the Blackburn works fully employed until the outbreak of the Second World War in September 1939. A Blackburn Skua was the first British aircraft to shoot down an enemy aircraft in World War Two; a Skua from HMS *Ark Royal* shot down a Dornier flying boat off Heligoland on 25 September 1939.

During the war years the Brough factory and other Blackburn plants at Dumbarton, Leeds and Sherburn-in-Elmet turned out a range of aircraft types including the Swordfish and the Firebrand both for the Fleet Air Arm as well as repairing damaged American aircraft. The end of the war however saw a decline in the company's fortunes and the need for Brough to undertake non-aviation work (even making bread tins for William Jackson's bakery!). In 1949 Blackburns merged with the General Aircraft Company based in Middlesex and this brought about an upturn in business. In the same year a new Universal Freighter Aircraft (later known as the Beverley) took to the skies. For twelve years the Beverley heavy freighter, remarkable for its sheer size as anyone who has seen the aircraft at Beverley's Museum of Army Transport will testify, was the RAF's 'heavy goods vehicle' all over the world.

Robert Blackburn's remarkable contribution to the history of aviation was marked in 1950 when at the age of 65 he was made Honorary Fellow of the Royal Aeronautical Society. However, after controlling the fortunes of the company for over forty years, health problems forced him to take a less active role. He retired to Devon but continued as chairman of the company. In this role he was well aware of an exciting new naval aircraft project which the company had embarked on: the Buccaneer twin-jet low-level strike aircraft for the Royal Navy. The project was top-secret but Robert Blackburn made guarded references to it at the Company's Annual General Meeting in August 1955 shortly before his death.

In his lifetime Robert Blackburn had seen his aircraft business grow from a tiny undertaking involving himself and two mechanics to a group of companies with over 5,000 employees. A career which had begun with designs inspired by the Wright Brothers and French aviation pioneers ended with jet aircraft like the Buccaneer at the cutting edge of technological innovation.

Blackburn's interest in sea-planes and the need to find somewhere to test them led him to choose this site close to the River Humber.

The Blackburn Beverley transport plane. (courtesy British Aerospace Heritage Centre, Brough, East Yorkshire)

9

Captain of Industry: Gordon Armstrong of Beverley (1885-1969)

Less than fifty years ago the engineering firm of Armstrong Patents was a familiar sight in Beverley. With factories in Eastgate and Swinemoor Lane the company was a major employer in the town. Once a household name in the manufacture of shock absorbers for the car industry the company was founded by Gordon Armstrong.

It is often an indication of the past importance of a local person to a town when a building, road or street is named after them. Anyone arriving in Beverley today might be intrigued by the existence of an Armstrong Way or an Armstrong's Social Club since substantial evidence of the person they are named after has long since vanished. Gordon Armstrong was not, in fact, a Beverlonian by birth: he was born in April 1885 at Border Rigg, Cumberland, of Anglo-Scottish parents. After serving an apprenticeship at an engineering firm in Gatesehead and attending classes at Gateshead Technical College he had a brief spell at sea as the fourth engineer on a ship working the North Atlantic route. The twenty-two year old Armstrong arrived in Beverley on January 1 1907. He had decided to set up in business as a motor engineer having acquired knowledge of the new internal combustion engine on the way. Armstrong rented a small engineering works, at Tiger Lane Beverley, for £8 a month and despite his lack of tools and equipment called his new business by the grand-sounding name of the East Riding Garage and Engineering Works. Although the motor trade was in its infancy Armstrong had chosen his career well for skilled motor engineers were in demand to repair and service the new and often temperamental 'horseless carriages'. The business prospered and Armstrong was able to expand his Tiger Lane premises to incorporate three shops and twelve cottages (which he converted into a large showroom and workshop) and to hire two mechanics and three apprentices. Armstrong's skill as an engineer was shown when, in 1909, he designed and built his own car and drove it to York. A second model of the 'Gordon' car was constructed and, in an era when building cars was still the job of a craftsman, contracts for building others (including orders from Australia and New Zealand) soon followed.

In 1910, three years after his arrival in Beverley, Armstrong was involved in another area of technological pioneering: that of aviation. The first powered flight, by the Wright Brothers, had only taken place seven years previously and flying was still both new and dangerous. Having witnessed aeroplanes in action at Doncaster, Armstrong decided to get his own and bought a Blériot monoplane for £20. Having fitted a 25 horsepower petrol engine into the machine Armstrong approached the authorities for permission to use Beverley Westwood for a trial flight.

A portrait of Gordon Armstrong by the Beverley painter, Fred Elwell.

On a Thursday evening, in the summer of 1910, Armstrong's plane was made ready for the flight witnessed, and hindered, by a large crowd that had assembled for the occasion. In the event no flight took place; in trying to start the engine Armstrong was injured when his left hand was struck by the propeller while there was a further mishap when, in trying to turn the machine, the back wheel buckled. Armstrong was forced to abandon his first attempt at flying complaining bitterly of the 'thoughtlessness of the crowd' although he was later able, unhindered by people, to get the machine into the air for about one hundred yards.

When the First World War began Armstrong turned his garage business over to the production of munitions and such was the demand for his howitzer shells that in 1917 he bought an old cart and wagon works in Eastgate, Beverley, to expand production. There seems little doubt that Gordon Armstrong was both a skilled engineer and a workaholic but the long hours that he put into the business took a severe toll of his health. When the First World War ended in 1918 he suffered a nervous breakdown. Such was the nature of the man, however, that his agile mind was still at work during his convalescence when he turned his thoughts to the subject of car comfort. In 1919 Armstrong invented a simple but effective shock absorber and this became the basis for the future success of his business. Further development of his shock absorber and that of independent wheel suspension during the 1920s and 1930s led to orders from the Ford Motor Company and, in 1929, from William Morris. At a time of depression and high unemployment in the early 1930s Armstrong's factory was a major success story in Beverley's economy. By the outbreak of the Second World War in September 1939 Armstrong's works in Eastgate were producing 4,000 shock absorbers a day and employing 450 workers. In addition, the earlier roots of his business, motor vehicles, were not neglected. Armstrong was an agent for Austin, Rover, Morris and Standard cars and to add to his business in North Bar Street Beverley, Armstrong built a large 24-hour garage at the junction of Anlaby Road and Boothferry Road in Hull. This opened in 1932. The success of Armstrong's businesses meant changes in his lifestyle: by 1936 he had moved from a house in York Road, Beverley, to Longcroft Hall and was also a

The former garage of Gordon Armstrong at the junction of Tiger Lane and North Bar Within, Beverley.

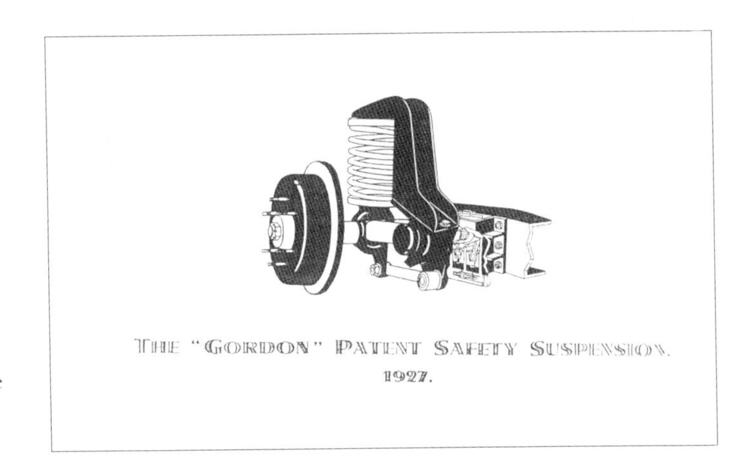

One of the car suspension systems that helped to make Armstrong's name and fortune.

Longcroft Hall, Beverley, home of Gordon Armstrong in the 1930s, is now part of Beverley College.

to indulge a passion for foreign travel and long sea voyages. Unfortunately during one of these, to South America in 1937, his wife Violet caught pneumonia and died on board the RMS *Laconia* at Rio de Janeiro.

With the coming of the Second World War the Eastgate factory was once more turned over to the production of munitions. Between 1939 and 1945 over 1,000 employees, both from Hull and Beverley, turned out a collection of products for the war effort ranging from tracer-shell casings for the Royal Navy to parts for Bofors guns. In many ways Armstrong was a progressive employer and a benefactor to Beverley and the war effort. He was one of the first employers in the country to introduce a five-day week for his workers and was active in providing money for the Beverley Cottage Hospital (1938). In the early stages of the war he was the first person in Britain to privately present an aircraft to the nation: a Hurricane fighter costing £8,500. Older Beverley residents may also remember the Pale Moon Café: a mobile canteen which Gordon Armstrong established in Beverley's market place and which served free cups of tea and coffee, day and night, to anyone in uniform. In 1940 he offered his home, Longcroft Hall, to the Ministry of Health, free of charge, for use as a hospital.

After the war Gordon Armstrong left the running of the business to his younger son, William Armstrong. By the mid 1950s the workforce was 2,500 and there were soon factories in Beverley, Hull and York; these were the boom years of the British car industry and Armstrong shock absorbers were much in demand. Gordon Armstrong retired to Weymouth in Dorset but remained the technical adviser to the firm. By 1968 Armstrong Patents had grown into a worldwide business with factories in Canada, Australia and South Africa. It is perhaps fortunate that Gordon Armstrong did not live to see the equally dramatic downturn of the business in the 1980s, which followed the catastrophic decline of British car industry. In 1981 the Eastgate Works closed with 300 redundancies while in 1989 the Armstrong business was sold to the American industrial giant Tenneco.

Gordon Armstrong died in Weymouth on July 30th 1969 aged eighty-four leaving, a considerable personal fortune of £98,423. His legacy for Beverley was also significant: as its foremost captain of industry, he made the town into a centre of component manufacture and brought both employment and prosperity to its people when both were sorely needed.

10

Down at Heel in Nineteenth Century Beverley: Life in the Workhouse

Until recent times the people of Beverley, as in other places, were generally expected make their own provision for times of sickness or for when they became too old to work. There were also other categories of people who, for no fault of their own, could not help themselves: orphans, the insane, deserted wives and the disabled. Unable to survive without support they might be look for help to family, to friends, or to charity.

In the Middle Ages the church was the major source of charity; Matthew, chapter 25, told the god-fearing to 'feed the hungry, clothe the naked and take in the stranger'. To this end the medieval church built hospitals; historically these were institutions to care for the poor and infirm. Beverley, by the mid-fifteenth century, had four church-run hospitals and this tradition of charity was carried on by private individuals in later times. Beverley became the home to several privately funded hospitals and almshouses. Ann Routh's hospital for widows, for example, was established in Keldgate in 1746 and housed thirty-two inmates while Sir Michael Warton's Hospital in Minster Moorgate had six poor widows who were allowed three shillings weekly with gowns and coals annually.

Private charity could not hope to deal with all paupers and by the seventeenth century parishes were made responsible for the problem. They could either provide 'outdoor relief' through cash allowances, fuel, clothing and food to paupers living at home or 'indoor relief' to the poor residing in a purpose-built workhouse. To lessen the cost of providing such a workhouse three Beverley parishes (St Martin, St Mary and St Nicolas) joined together to build one in Minster Moorgate in 1727. By the late eighteenth century this housed thirty or so paupers, mostly adult women and children, but the vast majority of those who obtained help did so through outdoor relief. The cost of poor relief was met by a tax on property values levied on the ratepayers of the parishes.

During the early nineteenth century national concern about the growing numbers of paupers and the increasing cost of poor relief led Parliament to pass the 1834 Poor Law. This combined parishes into unions and made indoor relief in a well-regulated workhouse the preferred way of dealing with all classes of paupers. To discourage all but the most desperate from applying, the Poor Law Commission in London hoped that life in each workhouse would be made deliberately hard. In the East Riding several new union workhouses were built including ones at Skirlaugh (1839), Driffield (1868) and at Beverley (1861). The new Beverley workhouse replaced the one in Minster Moorgate, by now considered inadequate to cope with the needs of the

Beverley Workhouse opened in 1861 and accommodated 189 inmates. It was built close to the Westwood and was designed by John and William Atkinson of York and built at a cost of over £5,000.

thirty-six parishes in the Beverley Poor Law Union. The red-brick, Tudor-style building for 189 inmates, built close to the Westwood, was designed by John and William Atkinson of York and built at a cost of over £5,000 (twice the estimate).

The aim of most Poor Law Guardians was to keep expenditure in check and so there were few luxuries. The food supplied, for example, was of the most basic kind; bread and gruel with occasional meat and potatoes. The story of the orphan, Oliver Twist, asking for more in the novel by Charles Dickens has a basis in fact!

After breakfast the children were sent to nearby schools while adults were expected to perform tasks such as breaking up cobbles, street sweeping and oakum picking (separating out the fibres of old ropes). Workhouse females performed the tasks involved in the day-today running of a large institution: preparing food, cooking, cleaning and washing.

In one case, at least, the harsh workhouse regime at Beverley seems to have deterred an application with fatal consequences. On the 25 January 1865 the East Riding coroner recorded a verdict of death by starvation on a widow called Eliza Smith (aged 60) of Woodmansey. The neighbour who found her told the inquest that Mrs Smith had no food in the house only 'some old bones which had been picked at and an apple or two'. The daughter of the deceased told the coroner that in the previous year her mother had applied to the Beverley Guardians for relief during the winter but had been refused unless she came into the workhouse. The inquest was told that the widow had refused the offer saying she would rather starve. The coroner suggested that the Beverley Guardians had been 'harsh' in not allowing the woman a 'few shillings in the winter after she strove to maintain herself in the summer'.

Above: The Workhouse in Minster Moorgate was first opened in 1727 but closed in 1861 when the new Union workhouse was opened on the edge of the Westwood. (courtesy Beverley Local Studies Library)

Below left: Oakum picking, separating the fibres of old ropes, was one of the tedious tasks given to workhouse inmates at Beverley.

Below right: A porter's lodge and archway over the entrance to the workhouse was added in 1895.

The Guardians' minute books of their monthly meetings show in stark detail the circumstances that drove Beverley's poor to apply for admittance to the workhouse. On the 31 March 1866, Ann McDougle appeared before the Guardians to say that her husband was refusing to maintain her (despite earning 30 shillings a week at a local foundry) and that she was destitute. The same day another woman, Ann Coates, told the Guardians that her husband (a joiner earning 24 shillings a week) had locked her out of the house and was refusing to maintain her. In both cases the women were admitted to the workhouse while the Guardians sought redress against their husbands by asking the Justices to issue warrants for their arrest 'for refusing to maintain their wives'.

In the interests of economy, and because much of the work could be done by the inmates themselves, the number of workhouse staff was small. An advertisement for a new master and matron in March 1867 shows that the Guardians wished to appoint a 'husband and wife, without family, between the ages of 25 and 50 years' for salaries of £55 and £25 respectively. The people appointed were James and Elizabeth Shives but they were soon judged to be incompetent and were asked to resign. At times these paid officials found it difficult to keep the inmates in order. Records show that in September 1866 Jane Wilson complained to the Board of Guardians that two other paupers, Ruth Blakeston and Mary Leighton, had struck her. In December 1868 the Workhouse Master complained about a fifteen year old boy who 'is very bad to manage and likely to corrupt the younger boys and influence them in disobedience'.

From the census records of the Beverley Workhouse it is clear that this institution combined the functions of an orphanage, old peoples' home, home for unmarried mothers, hospital and mental asylum in one building. The 1881 census, for example shows that that there were 156 residents including 5 described as 'imbeciles from birth'. The oldest resident was William Wilson (aged eighty-two) a former waterman of Beverley. At the other end of the age scale was Ellen Adams (aged two) whose mother, Mary Adams of North Newbald, was also resident in the workhouse.

The duty of the Beverley Board of Guardians, as they saw it, was to supervise the running of the workhouse and, for the benefit of the ratepayers, ensure that the system was run as economically as possible. Despite the intention to abolish outdoor relief this continued as before. In fact, the numbers who were given help in the form of money, food and clothes outside the workhouse always exceeded the numbers within it.

Although the Guardians were reluctant to spend public money unnecessarily, expensive improvements to the workhouse, usually prompted by critical inspection reports, were sometimes unavoidable. In 1893 a new infirmary with sixty beds was built while in 1895 a porter's lodge and archway over the road at the entrance to the workhouse were added. These changes, costing £8,000, provide a link between the original workhouse, use of the site (lasting until the 1930s) and its new role as a hospital beginning at the outbreak of the Second World War and continuing to the present day.

II

Trouble at the Mill: The Beverley Riot of 1861

Beverley's rapid growth in recent times has led to increasing concerns about the future of the town's historic pastures. The 1,200 acres which comprise the common lands of Swinemoor, Figham and, above all, the Westwood are seen, by some, as vulnerable to the kinds of housing development which have taken place elsewhere in the town. These fears have been heightened by the decline in the numbers of Pasture Masters, the body entrusted, since 1836, to manage the use of Beverley's most valuable leisure resource. The rights of Beverley's freemen and others to enjoy the blessings of the Westwood have been jealously guarded for centuries as the Corporation found to its cost in 1861.

Visitors to Beverley, arriving from Bishop Burton on the A1079, are invariably impressed by the breathtaking aspect given to the town by the magnificent Westwood Pastures. Few places in England can boast such a beautiful entrance to a town or provide its people with the opportunities for exercise, recreation and amusement as the Westwood. The rights of Beverley folk to use the Westwood date back to at least the fourteenth century. In 1380 Archbishop Neville of York granted the 'soil of the wood called Westwood' to the town forever on payment of £5 per year. Although most of the trees had disappeared by the sixteenth century (cut down to provide building materials or firewood) a remnant survives in the area of Burton Bushes; 26 acres of woodland on the western boundary. Since the 1380 Charter prohibited the use of the Westwood for arable farming its use was dominated by animal grazing. Within strictly controlled limits the freemen of the town could graze their cows and sheep while the town corporation made use of Westwood clay to make bricks and chalk as a foundation for Beverley's streets.

The corporation also granted the right to various individuals to lease sites and operate windmills on them. A familiar landmark on today's Westwood is the Black Mill, erected in 1803. The 65-year lease on the site had been granted by the Corporation in 1802 to Joseph Baitson at a rent of six guineas per year. Similarly in 1761 the corporation had granted a 99-year lease on a site close to the eastern boundary of the Westwood at Butt Close, adjoining St Giles Croft. Here on a mound a post-mill was erected with a masonry round-house at the base and a revolving wooden structure above containing the mill machinery and sails. In 1800 the lease was taken over by Robert Fishwick for a period of sixty years and he continued to operate the Dutch style windmill there.

The site of Fishwick's Mill was later to provide a major source of friction between the corporation and a group of the town's freemen. Until the nineteenth century it was the

Above: The Black Mill, erected in 1803. The 65-year lease on the site was granted by the Corporation in 1802 to Joseph Baitson at a rent of six guineas per year.

Opposite: A nineteenth-century pen and ink drawing of Fishwick's Mill by Caroline Brereton.

Corporation (elected by the freemen of the town) that granted leases for windmill sites. However, the passing of the Municipal Corporations Act in 1835 brought about an end to its powers over the Westwood and a new body of resident freemen (the Pasture Masters) was established, by law, to do the job. As the leases on windmill sites came to an end, the freemen were anxious to assert their authority and destroy these encroachments on their rights of pasture. In 1861 when the Fishwick lease came to an end the family dismantled their windmill but other buildings, including the mill-house remained. This issue was to bring a group of Beverley's freeman into direct conflict with the Corporation.

The trouble began around the end of August 1861 when some freemen began to pasture their cattle on the enclosed 1-acre site 'under the impression that the land was part and parcel of the common pasture'. Determined to assert their own position some members of the Corporation took it upon themselves to order the freemen off telling them they had no rights to the land and that it was the property of the Corporation. This, in turn, led to acts of vandalism with the result that three of the town's police force were ordered to stand guard. Together with the posting of notices warning that anyone found trespassing would be prosecuted, this act served to inflame the situation since a large number of freemen believed that they had been cheated of their rights.

On Monday 2 September 1861 John Duffill, bellman, went around the town urging the freemen to gather at the mill site that evening to take possession of it. Around 7 p.m. a large crowd 'of all ages and both sexes' gathered to confront the few police on duty. When Duffill demanded entrance, and was refused, he took matters into his own hands and jumped over the gate, quickly followed by the rest. The police, heavily outnumbered, then decided to withdraw, no doubt aware if fighting ensued that the piles of bricks lying around the site would provide the crowd with a plentiful supply of ammunition. Although many of those who took part in the protest were freemen of the town it seems likely that other elements used the opportunity for mischief making. Among those who gathered there were two or three juveniles, about ten or twelve years old, who when asked what business they had there replied: 'We are freemen of Beverley and have come to take our rights!'

Some of the crowd, however, were determined to go further than peaceful protest and, in the words of one local newspaper, carried out 'an outrage that will prove a lasting disgrace'. They broke into the mill house, smashed the windows, knocked out the window frames, doors and shutters and at about 8 o'clock set fire to the building. As the fire burned it was said 'those involved in the incendiary act threw bricks at the red hot, tottering walls in order to bring them down'. While this was going on other rioters were engaged in destroying trees and plants and sawing down the thorn hedge which separated the site from the surrounding pasture.

The Corporation was determined not to let the actions of those responsible go unpunished. Alderman Robson summed up the feelings of many when he said that there was a need to defend the property of the borough from the 'lawless depredations of a certain class of men and to bring the ringleaders to justice'. Another of the Conservative majority, Alderman Arden, suggested that the whole outrage had been 'concocted in some public house in the town and that the riotous proceedings had been premeditated'.

Championing the cause of the freemen however was Cllr Hind who commented on the Corporation's inconsistent approach. He asked how the Corporation, having given up the rents of the other Westwood mills, could expect to retain this one? His appeal to reason, however, fell on deaf ears and the motion to prosecute the ringleaders was carried by fourteen votes to three (9 September 1861).

Proceedings against those involved first began on September 21 1861 with an accusation of riot against John Duffill and fifteen others. The five magistrates having listened to the police evidence about 2 September decided that there was a case to answer and committed the defendants to trial at the next quarter sessions. A week later another batch of delinquents (as a local newspaper described them) appeared before three magistrates accused of the destruction of a house in the occupation of John Fishwick. Francis William Boyes and thirteen others were charged with 'maliciously injuring a dwelling house and premises on the Westwood belonging to the Corporation'.

In fact, given the weight of evidence against Boyes and the rest, the Corporation could have demanded that they be punished severely but chose not to do so. Perhaps to avoid a public backlash the Corporation declared, through their counsel, that they had 'no vindictive feeling in the matter' and hoped that the Bench would deal with the defendants as leniently as possible. The magistrates, it seemed, took this advice. Only five out of the fourteen accused were found guilty and even their punishment was relatively light. They were each fined six shillings for the damage and had to pay costs of fourteen shillings. Satisfied with the five convictions, and perhaps to draw a line under the entire affair, the Corporation then agreed to drop all further charges.

The violent events of September 1861 helps us to understand the tensions which existed in the town in the mid-nineteenth century between the poorer class of freemen and those wealthy and influential enough to wield political power. The freemen showed, by their determined stand over the issue of the Fishwick Mill site, that their rights and wishes could not be ignored. Ultimately they were the victors too, since the land on which the mill had stood did revert back to being part of the Westwood again. In the nineteenth century the pasture freemen numbered over 1,400, in marked contrast to today when there are less than 180. The closure of the Westwood Maternity Hospital in recent times has put the long-term future of the Pasture Masters in doubt and has contributed to the anxieties of those who see a development threat to the town's pastures.

12

Gone To Blazes: East Yorkshire Fire Fighting Through the Ages

In the twenty-first century we often take for granted that, in an emergency, we can rely on professionally trained and well-equipped public services to come to our aid. The Humberside Fire and Rescue Service covering over a thousand square miles of East Yorkshire and Northern Lincolnshire responds to over 20,000 incidents every year ranging from chip-pan fires in the home to major incidents like Beverley's Bartoline inferno of May 2003. The skilled personnel and specialised equipment of a modern fire service is however a far cry from the more primitive arrangements that existed in the past.

For many centuries the towns and villages of the East Riding had no organised way of fighting fires and relied on basic equipment such as leather buckets, hooks and grappling irons. If a fire took hold in the timber and thatch dwellings of the past often the only way of stopping it spreading was to create fire-breaks by pulling down neighbouring houses using a crook and chain. Following the Great Fire of London in 1666 when huge areas of the capital were laid waste it seems that the authorities in Beverley began to take the risk more seriously and ordered the purchase of buckets and fire hooks. Before the advent of professional fire-fighting volunteers had to be summoned to deal with blazes by the ringing of church bells. To encourage this aspect of citizenship Beverley Corporation, in 1681, gave rewards to those people who attended a fire. They also sought to deter, through fines, a lack of care by Beverley tradesmen using candles near combustible materials. In January 1738 they ordered that any person 'dressing flax by candlelight or carrying a lighted candle where flax is' should be fined 10 shillings. This was a large sum by eighteenth-century standards and reflected the Corporation's concern that 'there had been several fires of late in the town from this cause'.

The fire hazards of carrying on a trade were also evident in East Riding villages. In May 1711 Matthew Borman of Leven suffered a fire that began in his blacksmith's shop and spread next door to the carpenter's shop of Thomas Newton.

In an age of open fires and lighted candles there was also a high risk of domestic fires being started by accident. Records show how a careless servant of Marmaduke Ward of Aike (near Beverley) had, in 1748, caused a fire by sweeping ashes from a fire onto straw laid on the floor of his master's house. To deter such carelessness an act of 1774 warned servants that if their actions led to the destruction of a house they faced a fine of £100 or 18 months imprisonment with hard labour.

From the eighteenth century there were some limited improvements in the technology of fighting fires through the introduction of fire engines. Beverley's first engine, it seems, arrived in

Above: Cottingham Fire Brigade, composed of sixteen volunteers, was formed in around 1887.

Opposite above: Beverley's old fire station, housed in the former drill hall in Albert Terrace, Beverley is now a doctors' surgery.

Opposite below: Beverley's modern fire station in New Walkergate opened in 1983.

1725 thanks to the generosity of a local resident called Fotherby. Beverley Corporation thanked him for his gift and went on to order the employment of twelve people to work the engine on a casual basis and to be 'ready and diligent upon all occasions when a fire shall happen'. In 1831 it became necessary to buy a new engine and so one was ordered from Simpkin and Loft of London that was capable of 'ejecting two bodies of water in different directions with great force'. In order to pay for the engine a subscription was organised with an appeal for funds being made to residents of the town and to fire insurance companies like Norwich and the Phoenix (who each subscribed £10). Fire insurance was a lucrative business and, to encourage those who could afford it, insurance companies provided customers with 'Fire Marks' to fix to the walls of their houses to indicate that they had cover. One of these can still be seen on Tymperon House in Beverley's Walkergate.

Throughout much of the nineteenth century, fighting fires continued to rely a great deal on voluntary effort and in an age of horse-drawn fire appliances this had to be local. Some communities made more effort than others. Beverley had a volunteer brigade by 1885 while the Cottingham Fire Brigade, composed of sixteen volunteers, was formed around 1887. It operated from a station house in Northgate using an engine provided by the Cottingham Local Board

BEVERLEY FIRE STATION

and horses loaned by local residents. In the brigade's first annual report (March 1888) the captain of the volunteers, Charles Naylor, recorded how the Cottingham engine had only attended four fires but had been out 'twenty times on drills and practices'. Naylor, who by day was the station-master of Cottingham railway station, asserted that his men had been 'thoroughly well drilled during the summer evenings' to encourage them to be smart at their work.

By the late nineteenth century local authorities had the power to meet the expenditure of maintaining a fire brigade from local taxation and many used this opportunity. Sometimes authorities would join together to minimise the costs involved. In 1912, for example, Driffield's Urban and Rural District Councils established a joint brigade and purchased one of the newly developed motor fire engines. Since they were paying the costs involved, the joint committee laid down charges for fighting fires outside their own area. For the use of their new fire engine they charged non-residents 5 guineas for the first hour!

As Chief Officer of the joint Fire Brigade they chose John Alton and decided to pay him a retaining fee of £15 per year while the other eight retained firemen would each get one pound. Within a year of taking up his post it seems that Alton was at odds with the chairman of the Fire Brigade Committee, Cllr Ullyott, and his resignation was called for. However, Alton stood his ground and wrote to the committee claiming that he broken none of the rules of the brigade or done anything to warrant his resignation. It seems the committee agreed with him for his position as Chief Officer was confirmed by four votes to two! A clash of personalities between Alton and Ullyott is indicated by the fact that Alton was soon looking elsewhere for employment and in February 1914 was appointed as Engineer of the Western Australian Fire Board.

Back in Beverley the volunteer fire brigade continued until 1924 (with financial support from Beverley Corporation) when a new professional force of nine firemen was established. In the same year the corporation bought a motor fire engine and a fire station was constructed using unused police cells at Beverley's Guildhall. The brigade was to fight all fires in the borough and also served Beverley Rural District Council.

Further changes were to follow during the years of the Second World War when all of the East Riding's independent brigades became part of the National Fire Service under the control of the Home Office. After the war the need for efficiency and professionalism led to the formation of the East Riding Fire Brigade. To serve Beverley and places nearby a fire station was established at a former drill hall at Albert Terrace in Beverley. This Old Fire Station was, in turn, replaced by purpose-built premises in New Walkergate which opened in 1983.

The Beverley fire station is today complemented by others scattered across the huge operational area of Humberside Fire and Rescue including those at Driffield, Bridlington, Sledmere, Market Weighton and Pocklington and these are largely staffed by retained firefighters. Following national trends an important part of the strategy of today's fire service is Community Fire Safety with the aim being to reduce the number of fires and fire casualties. To this end Humberside Fire and Rescue seeks to change attitudes to fire prevention and detection by householders and encourage them to make an escape plan should a fire break out.

13

A Racing Certainty: Three Centuries of the Sport of Kings at Beverley

Yorkshire has many attractions to offer and horse racing is one that brings large numbers of people to the county each year. The county boasts some of the finest race courses in England, none more so than Beverley, set amidst the splendour of the town's historic Westwood Pastures. The story of Beverley Races dates back over three centuries.

The vast crowds drawn to Beverley's racecourse each season are in marked contrast to the simple beginnings of the sport during the seventeenth century. It is likely that local owners were in the habit of 'matching' their horses on the town's pastures long before there was any formal event. However, the origins of the racecourse can be traced back to September 1690 when Beverley Corporation gave permission for a course on the Westwood 'where it had lately been used'. This racecourse seems to have been in the area of the Black Mill where the 'Tan Gallop' is now situated. From about 1765 the present racecourse, in Hurn Pasture, came into use.

By 1712 the Beverley Races took place on three days in September but within a short time May had become the preferred month. The races grew in popularity thanks to the support of the town's MPs and the encouragement of publicans who, to the exclusion of outsiders, did a brisk trade on race days. This fact was recognised, in 1730,by Beverley Corporation who ordered that 'for the encouragement of the horse races' every innholder wanting to set up a stall on the Westwood had to pay 5 shillings (25p). By 1742 those selling wine had to pay 10s 6d (53p), those selling beer 5 shillings and, to ensure that only local inhabitants benefited from the business opportunities that racing brought, it was stated that Beverley people alone could set up booths for the sale of alcohol.

The Corporation took a keen interest in the progress of the event and this is shown by numerous entries in their minute books. On the 17 March 1743, for example, it was recorded that William Agar was chosen to look after the race flags, to weigh the riders and 'to have fifteen shillings for his trouble'. The sale of alcohol at race events meant that there was a need to keep good order and deter rowdy behaviour; in July 1728 it was recorded that the constables should receive three guineas for their attendance at the races. Since most spectators at this time did not pay to watch, the races had to be supported by those wealthy and willing enough to make a financial contribution. In 1784, for example, Sir Christopher Sykes, one of Beverley's MPs, promised to pay £25 and in the nineteenth century Beverley Corporation pledged regular subscriptions in support of the races.

By 1763 racing took place on three days in June and a notice of that time shows that the

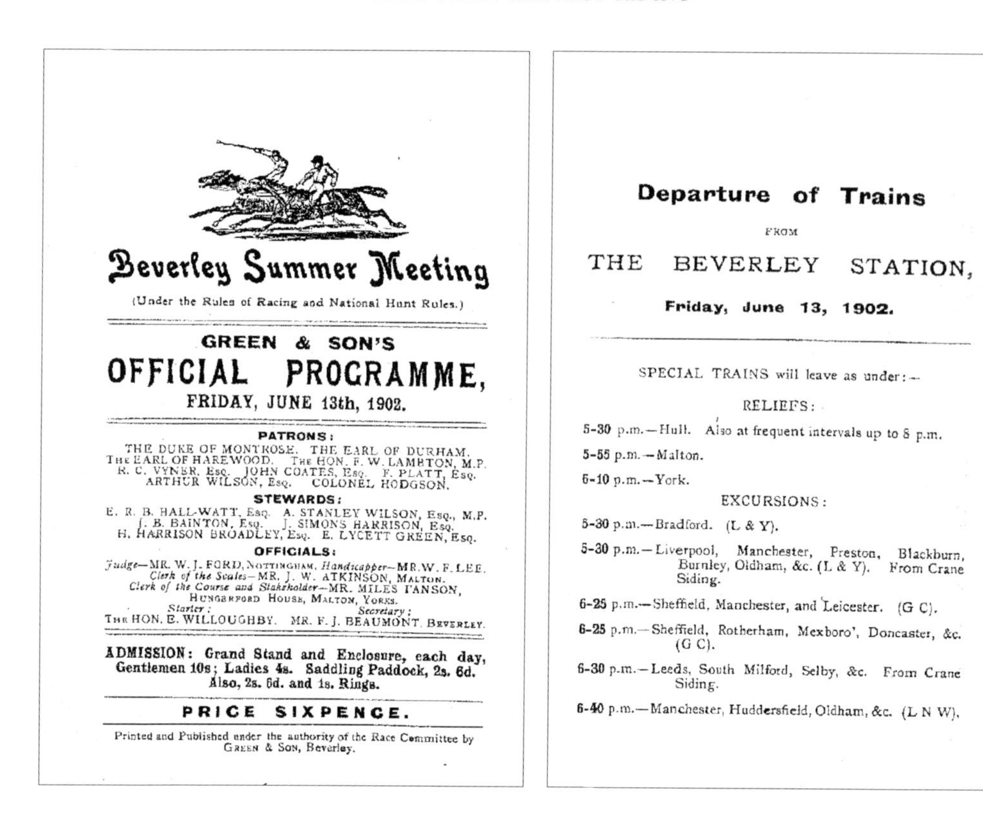

Beverley Summer Meeting

(Under the Rules of Racing and National Hunt Rules.)

GREEN & SON'S

OFFICIAL PROGRAMME,

FRIDAY, JUNE 13th, 1902.

PATRONS:

THE DUKE OF MONTROSE. THE EARL OF DURHAM.
THE EARL OF HAREWOOD. THE HON. F. W. LAMBTON, M.P.
R. C. VYNER, Esq. JOHN COATES, Esq. F. PLATT, Esq.
ARTHUR WILSON, Esq. COLONEL HODGSON.

STEWARDS:

E. R. B. HALL-WATT, Esq. A. STANLEY WILSON, Esq., M.P.
J. B. BAINTON, Esq. J. SIMONS HARRISON, Esq.
H. HARRISON BROADLEY, Esq. E. LYCETT GREEN, Esq.

OFFICIALS:

Judge—MR. W. J. FORD, NOTTINGHAM. *Handicapper*—MR. W. F. LEE.
Clerk of the Scales—MR. J. W. ATKINSON, MALTON.
Clerk of the Course and Stakeholder—MR. MILES I'ANSON,
HUNGERFORD HOUSE, MALTON, YORKS.
Starter: THE HON. E. WILLOUGHBY. *Secretary*: MR. F. J. BEAUMONT, BEVERLEY.

ADMISSION: Grand Stand and Enclosure, each day, Gentlemen 10s; Ladies 4s. Saddling Paddock, 2s. 6d. Also, 2s. 6d. and 1s. Rings.

PRICE SIXPENCE.

Printed and Published under the authority of the Race Committee by GREEN & SON, Beverley.

Departure of Trains

FROM

THE BEVERLEY STATION,

Friday, June 13, 1902.

SPECIAL TRAINS will leave as under:—

RELIEFS:

5-30 p.m.—Hull. Also at frequent intervals up to 8 p.m.

5-55 p.m.—Malton.

6-10 p.m.—York.

EXCURSIONS:

5-30 p.m.—Bradford. (L & Y).

5-30 p.m.—Liverpool, Manchester, Preston, Blackburn, Burnley, Oldham, &c. (L & Y). From Crane Siding.

6-25 p.m.—Sheffield, Manchester, and Leicester. (G C).

6-25 p.m.—Sheffield, Rotherham, Mexboro', Doncaster, &c. (G C).

6-30 p.m.—Leeds, South Milford, Selby, &c. From Crane Siding.

6-40 p.m.—Manchester, Huddersfield, Oldham, &c. (L N W).

A race programme from 1902. Note the large umber of special excursion trains to Beverley Races. (courtesy of East Riding Archives Service)

event had taken on a wider social significance for the town with 'an Assembly every night during the races at the New Assembly Rooms'. Of a less civilised nature were the cockfights that were arranged 'every morning during the Races between the gentlemen of Hull and the gentlemen of the East Riding for four guineas a battle'. For the comfort of affluent race-goers grandstands were approved in 1767 and 1769. One of the people active in support of the races was Sir James Pennyman who lived at the Hall in Beverley's Lairgate. Pennyman employed the architect John Carr from York to design a grandstand and also contributed to its cost.

During the nineteenth century the coming of the railway helped to swell the numbers attending Beverley Races and made it easier to transport horses from further afield. A newspaper report of June 1858 records that most of the horses for the Beverley meeting of 16/17 June arrived by train from Driffield while on the first day of the meeting there were, for race-goers, 'cheap excursion trains on the Hull and Scarborough line and a train from Leeds conveying passengers there and back for 2s 6d'. This same local reporter commented that the Wednesday meeting had eight races and claimed that this was 'rather formidable for a place like Beverley'. He complained about the lack of punctuality in running the races at the time stated on the card and said that this was 'fast becoming an intolerable nuisance'. The Beverley reporter argued that with the races finishing at 7 p.m., rather than the advertised 6 p.m., this prevented 'many visitors from distant localities seeing the termination of the sport'.

The imposing entrance to the racecourse viewed from York Road.

Race Day at Beverley, May 2006. (courtesy Nick Wright)

There seems little doubt that the presence of the racecourse served to stimulate the economy of the town. The Corporation, in 1735, had decided that racehorses from any part of the country could run there but that they should be brought to the town at least seven days before the race. This meant, of course, that owners would have to spend money on stable fees for their horses and accommodation costs for themselves!

Nearby villages also benefited from the Beverley Races. The Bishop Burton public house, the Altisidora, is a reminder of the success of the racehorse of that name in the St Leger of 1813. Squire Watt of Bishop Burton bred and trained Altisidora and numerous successful racehorses in the early nineteenth century. One of these was the mare Nancy jointly owned with the Beverley trainer Thomas Lister. A newspaper report of June 1851 records that Lister had been adding to his stock of horses by purchasing four yearlings from 'the celebrated stud at Meaux Abbey of Mr Richardson. The Tan Gallop to the south of the racecourse was made as a training circuit for horses around 1870 and records show that the Pasture Masters benefited from fees of £1 15s 0d per horse from the forty-one horses using it in 1890. A Beverley Directory of 1892 illustrates racing's impact on the town since it lists five people who were described as racehorse trainers. At the turn of the century some of these trainers, like John Whipp and Isaac Cook, lived at Willow Grove on the edge of the Westwood. These dwellings had the advantage that they were close to the racing stables in York Road (adjacent to the Rose and Crown Public House). The 1901 census also shows us the existence of the jockeys Abraham Batty who lived at Hobson's Yard, North Bar, Within and James Wheatley, who lived at No. 40 New Walk.

The growth of racing at Beverley was helped by the fact that the much larger city of Hull was not able to establish a long-term venue of its own. Meetings had been held at Anlaby Road (then outside the Hull boundary) between 1750 and 1796 and a new Hull racecourse, at Hedon, operated between 1888 and 1909. However, in both cases they failed to survive. At the turn of the twentieth century the future of the Beverley Racecourse itself, though not the races, seemed uncertain. In 1902 the tenancy agreement with the Beverley Pasture Masters was in doubt and in view of the uncertainty the Beverley and East Riding Race Company was not able 'to make the necessary extensions and improvements to bring the meetings up-to-date'. As a consequence plans were made for a new racecourse at Broadgate Farm, near Walkington, for a yearly rent of £475. In the event these plans were not implemented since a new arrangement was made with the Pasture Masters on the future of the existing racecourse.

With the cooperation of the Pasture Masters the further development of the racecourse now became possible. In 1925 the old stone-built grandstand of 1767 was dismantled to make way for more up-to date facilities while in 1935 more of the course became enclosed so that admission-paying public areas could be created and the financial security of racing strengthened. Beverley Races were suspended during the years of the Second World War when the racecourse was under military occupation but resumed in 1946.

The period since the war has seen the most remarkable changes at the course in its long history. New stands were built in 1959 and 1967 and these together with further building work during the 1990s created more luxurious facilities for owners, trainers and public alike (including a new weighing room complex opened in 1998). These improvements to the course together with improved marketing strategies (like the Works Night Out introduced in 2003) have helped to win the approval of new generations of racing enthusiasts and boost attendance figures. Under the guidance of Sally Iggulden, Britain's youngest ever racecourse manager, the fortunes of Beverley Races seemed set for further growth in the years to come.

14

Britain's Oldest Horse Race: The Kiplingcotes Derby

In March each year, as Winter gives way to Spring, a traditional horse racing event, dating back almost five centuries, takes place amid the scenic grandeur of the Yorkshire Wolds. The Kiplingcotes Derby, with its origins in Tudor times, is reputed to be Britain's oldest flat race. Governed by eccentric, time-honoured rules it is a fascinating reminder of a by-gone age and provides a strenuous test of endurance for both horses and riders.

Racing enthusiasts unfamiliar with East Yorkshire and arriving for the annual Kiplingcotes Derby (held, by tradition, on the third Thursday in March) will search in vain for signs of a racecourse in the modern sense of the word. They will find no grandstand, no parade-ring, no winner's enclosure and no entrance fee! In fact the Kiplingcotes course, four miles of farm lanes, grass verges and tracks, only sees one race in the entire year. Run more like a point-to-point but without the fences, it is reputed that the race began in 1519 during the reign of Henry VIII. The first written evidence about it dates from 1556.

The Kiplingcotes Derby probably had its origins as an event for the East Riding gentry who wished to match their horses after the long winter months. The race seems to have become important enough by 1619 to have become endowed with funds by leading figures of the day including the Earl of Burlington, Sir John Hotham and Sir Marmaduke Constable. Together forty-nine benefactors provided an investment fund that generated an income for prize money. In 1822 this fund stood at £468 and the interest the money earned paid a first prize of at least £15. The founders also drew up rules for the good management of the event. These articles, for example, stipulated that: 'every horse that runs for the prize shall start bridled and saddled and shall run with the rider weighing 10 stone.'

A shortened version of these old rules is still read out to the competitors by the clerk of the course around 11.30 a.m. on the day of the race. The riders are warned that any who 'hold or strike another will not win a prize'. The clerk of the course also checks on the weight of the riders, before and after the race, using a coal-merchants scale brought to the course for the purpose. Since 1980 Susan Hillaby, following on the tradition of her father and grandfather, has carried out these duties and kept the race's traditions alive. Any rider under the weight limit can make up the shortfall by carrying weights in their clothes. In the year 2000, for example, the weight rule meant that Laura Crawford (the winner of the previous year's event) had to carry two stones of sand in her clothing! Other riders have been known to wear spanners, tyre levers and other tools to make up their weight to the required level. Neither can the riders afford to

The famous Kiplingcotes winning post. (courtesy Colin Westley)

lose weight during the race; in 1961 one rider lost most of her lead weights from her pockets and weighed in 11lbs lighter than the required 10 stone. The lady in question was disqualified even though she passed the winning post first !

Another of the peculiarities of the 'Derby' is that the riders are weighed in and pay their entry fee of £4.25 at the finishing post before the race starts. In keeping with the quaint traditions of the race no one knows how many horses and riders will turn up until the race day itself and the numbers who compete vary widely from year to year. The 2006 Kiplingcotes Derby (run on 16 March) had nine runners and riders but other years have seen far fewer. The 2001 outbreak of foot-and-mouth disease led to the cancellation of the race proper although to keep the tradition alive, one official entrant was allowed to ride the course alone. Although this might seem bizarre, according to Kiplingcotes unwritten rules the race is permanently cancelled if the organisers miss a year. In fact, the 2001 'one-horse-race' was not without precedent: in 1947 when the course was covered in deep snow it was left to Fred Stephenson on Londesborough Lad to keep the racing tradition alive. Stephenson lived near the winning post and forced his way through snowdrifts, four feet deep in places, to reach the starting point, four and a half miles away. The 'Derby' took him an hour and twenty minutes to complete instead of the more usual ten minutes but, as he told reporters, 'I only rode to keep the famous race going'.

There is little doubt that a combination of terrain, thick pulling mud and bad weather can make the Kiplingcotes Derby a major trial for both horses and riders. After completing the weighing formalities and listening to the rules of the race the riders make their way to the start point, a sandstone post one mile north of the old Kiplingcotes railway station. It is an indication

Right: Ken Holmes, the Galloping Granddad, is an equine dentist from Selby. He has won the Kiplingcotes Derby ten times but in 2006 announced that this was to be his final race. (courtesy Johnathan Palmer)

Below: A quaint tradition of the race is that the rules are first read to the contenders at the finishing post before horses make their way to the start post four and a half miles away! (courtesy Johnathan Palmer)

The winner's trophy. (courtesy Johnathan Palmer)

of the strenuous nature of the challenge facing them that the starting post is 160 feet above sea level while the finishing post is 450 feet. Adding to their burden is the unpredictable March weather with cold biting winds, stinging rain and snow. Under these gruelling conditions the four-and-a-half mile course can take its toll of the entrants and in 1966 and 1979 horses collapsed at the end of the race and died.

One of the most successful of the Kiplingcotes contestants in recent times has been Ken Holmes a seventy-four year-old equine dentist from Selby and known affectionately as the Galloping Granddad. His name first appeared on the winner's list in 1983 and by 2006 (which he declared was his final appearance) he had won the race ten times. In 2006 the race, watched by 500 spectators, was won by the nineteen year-old Katie Croft on a thirteen year-old grey called Etton Lad.

The glory involved in winning England's oldest horse race is in fact far greater than any monetary reward for another peculiarity of the rules is that the winner has frequently received less prize money than the runner-up! This came about because the prize for being first was generated from the interest on the invested funds of trustees while the prize for runner-up was derived from the entrance fee of £4.25. In the year 2000, for example, with eighteen riders taking part the entrance fees gave second-place rider Ken Holmes a prize of £72 while the winner, Fiona Nixon of Easington, only received £50 (together with a trophy).

It is the quaint and seemingly incomprehensible features of the Kiplingcotes Derby which make the event such a well loved part of East Yorkshire's heritage and explains why riders and spectators loyally return to take part in this 'living history' spectacle each year.

15

A Festival of Country Living: 150 years of the Driffield Show

A reaction against the dominance of supermarkets in recent times has seen the growth of farmers' markets around the country, including East Yorkshire. By bringing producers and customers more directly together these markets are a return to the important old links that once existed between farmers and the wider community. The Driffield Show, which began over 150 years ago, was one such link.

Among the many summer delights in the country calendar, the county show must rank as a major highlight. The Driffield Show has long been pre-eminent in the East Riding as both a business and social event and in the year 2004 it celebrated its 150th birthday.

The origins of the Driffield Show can be traced back to the late eighteenth century when farming was undergoing profound changes. An interest in more scientific methods of agriculture and in improved farming methods led to the formation of local societies to promote new ideas. One such local agricultural society was in existence at by 1794; this was the forerunner of a 'Farmers Club' which in 1851 began organising local demonstrations of farm machinery. The interest in these events led to the formation of the Driffield and East Riding Agricultural Society in 1853. From the outset this new body planned to hold an annual agricultural show and the first of these was held on Wednesday 12 July 1854 in two fields adjoining Kingsmill Lane, Driffield. The occasion received extensive coverage in the *Farmer's Magazine* of the time which declared that the 'quantity and quality of cattle, sheep, pigs, poultry, horses and implements exhibited far surpassed expectations'. The entrance fee in the morning was 2s 6d, falling to 1 shilling by noon and 3d by mid-afternoon. These prices brought the show within means of most people and over 6,000 attended the event. The success of this first show led to more ambitious preparations for a second one with displays of machinery and fertilisers designed to encourage 'innovation and experimentation' among the farming community. The 1855 show was followed by a dinner at the Corn Exchange presided over by Lord Hotham. Among those entertained were the competition judges who had come from as far afield as Newcastle, Mansfield and Sheffield.

The Driffield Show quickly became established as an annual event; the town's expanding communications links (for example the Malton-Driffield Railway, opened in 1855) brought in both visitors and manufacturers from further afield. The event also ceased to be merely an agricultural show and took on a wider cultural significance as an event for the whole community with fairground attractions, stalls and musical entertainment. In 1867 there was a change of venue with the show being held in four fields on Beverley Lane (now St John's Road).

The horticulture tent at the Driffield Show is a popular visitor attraction. (courtesy John Richardson)

At the 1867 show there were 286 horses on display and the growing national reputation of the event is indicated when the prize for the best hunter went to Thomas Gee who had travelled from Wadhurst in Sussex to be there.

By 1887 the annual July extravaganza was being called 'The Great Show of the Riding' and the excitement generated by it was shown in a newspaper report of that year's event. This said 'by breakfast time the streets were thronged with country folk, beribboned and beflowered horses, stalls of itinerant goody men, ice cream vendors, shooting galleries, Aunt Sallies, try your strengths and other attractions'. In the following year, despite some apprehension about the wet weather, the show was honoured by the attendance of a member of the British royal family. Prince Albert Victor arrived by train from Bridlington for a procession by horse-drawn carriage along streets thronged with people 'amid the waving of handkerchiefs by the numerous ladies who had congregated'. Spanning the street near the Buck Hotel was 'an imposing triumphal arch of evergreens interwoven with flowers and bedecked with flags' built in honour of the royal visitor.

However, the newspapers of the time commented that the industry which had been the mainstay of the show, agriculture, had fallen on hard times. By the late nineteenth century British farming faced stiff competition from emerging countries like the USA, Canada and Australia and the 1888 newspaper report commented that 'the proceedings after the show were not of a very exhilarating character, not like the palmy days before the agricultural depression set in'.

There is little doubt that this depression did have an adverse effect on the fortunes of the show and its organisers for the attendance numbers did not always cover the costs of the event. For

Above left: A brass token given as a prize at the first Driffield show in 1854.

Above right: Exhibiting animals has always been an important part of the Driffield show.

a time, shortly before the outbreak of the First World War, it appeared that financial problems might bring an end both to the Driffield and East Riding Agricultural Society and to the Driffield Show. In the event enough sponsors came forward to save them although the show itself was suspended during the war years and did not resume until 1920.

In the inter-war period the continuing depression in farming still had an adverse effect and the event was again suspended between 1931 and 1936. Following personnel changes in 1937 and the arrival of more enthusiasts into key positions the show was once more revived and, except for the years of the Second World War, has been held ever since. In the late 1940s and early 1950s the Driffield Show grew in popularity: the 1949 show held on the Bridlington Road Show Ground, had fifty-one trade stands on display as well as 'George the Giant', the largest bullock in the world! With increasing attendance figures the Driffield Agricultural Society decided (in 1952) to buy its own permanent showground. This was at Kelleythorpe on the western outskirts of the town and the fifty-one acre site was levelled, drained and prepared in record time for the official opening by Lord Halifax in July 1953. Despite the fact that the show day was one of grey skies over 8,000 people paid for admission, there were over one thousand cars in the car parks and eighty trade stands in attendance.

Fifty years later the Driffield Show's traditional attractions of show jumping, competitions to find the 'best-of-breed', displays of farm machinery and stands of local food producers remain. To emphasise the continuing importance of farming in the local community the 2006 show had a display called 'Wheat to Bread' to explain the processes involved from the basic raw material to the finished product.

Although the needs of farming remain a priority for Driffield's annual one-day event other attractions have been added. These days an 'Enterprise Village' shows how farming can diversify into a range of new businesses while horticulture handicraft, retail and motoring stands meet the needs and interests of a wider range of show-goers.

The Driffield Show remains a popular event attracting attendances in excess of 20,000. Furthermore the Kelleythorpe Show Ground has become an important asset to the town with numerous other events staged there throughout the year ranging from motor home shows to gun dog trials.

16

Stand and Deliver: Dick Turpin in East Yorkshire

One of the more enduring myths of history is that of the 'gentleman of the road' – the highwayman. From the realms of fiction, rather than fact, we envisage a romantic and dashing figure on horseback, ambushing unwary travellers with a cry of 'stand and deliver'. Of all the highwaymen who plagued England's roads in the eighteenth century none is better known than Dick Turpin. The legend, however, bears little resemblance to the reality of the sordid criminal whose career came to a dramatic conclusion in the Brough area of East Yorkshire.

A key factor in the transformation of Dick Turpin from ruffian to hero was the nineteenth-century fiction writer Harrison Ainsworth. In his novel *Rookwood,* published in 1834, he depicted Turpin as a bold, devil-may-care figure who, on his horse Black Bess, made a legendary ride from London to York in less than twenty-four hours. In fact Ainsworth had stolen the idea of this ride from the exploits of another highwayman called John Nevison who had apparently made such a journey in 1676 to establish an alibi for one of his own robberies.

The historical figure that was the real Richard Turpin was altogether a more mean, brutal and callous individual. He was born in Essex around the year 1705, the son of John Turpin a local farmer and publican. Having received an education of sorts, he was apprenticed to a butcher at Whitechapel, then on the outskirts of London. After setting up in the butchery trade Turpin began stealing sheep and cattle to supply his business but was caught and had to flee into the Essex countryside to evade punishment. By late 1734 Turpin had joined Samuel Gregory and a band of desperados who became known as the Essex Gang. The group specialised in breaking into lonely farmhouses and terrorising the female occupants into handing over their money and valuables. Turpin's vicious nature is indicated by a raid at Loughton in Essex when he held an old widow woman over an open fire until she agreed to tell them where her valuables were hidden.

By 1735 a reward of £50 had been offered for the capture of the Essex Gang and after further violent crimes this was increased to £100. The promised reward may have helped to secure the arrest of two of its members at an ale-house in Westminster. Turpin, it is said, only escaped by leaping through a window and went on the run by becoming a highwayman and joining forces with another of his kind, Tom King.

Their main focus of activity seems to have been the roads around Epping Forest and Hampstead Heath. From a cave on the King's Oak and Loughton road the pair would swoop down on unsuspecting travellers. By 1737 the activities of Turpin and King had become so notorious that a further reward of £100 was on offer. This small fortune led a local gamekeeper, Thomas

The traditional image of Dick Turpin, highwayman, from a nineteenth-century engraving.

Morris, to travel to Epping Forest to track Turpin down. The highwaymen were determined to resist capture and on 4 May 1737 Turpin shot Morris dead. As a result of the murder the hunt for Turpin intensified; the descriptions issued said he was broad about the shoulders and 'much marked by smallpox'.

With pressure increasing in the London area Turpin made his escape northwards and it was now that the East Yorkshire phase of his criminal career began. To escape detection Richard Turpin now adopted the alias of John Palmer (the second name his mother's maiden name) and halted his journey north at Long Sutton in Lincolnshire. Here he was involved, for a few months, in horse-stealing, sheep rustling and, perhaps, highway robbery. As complaints about him grew he moved again and, by early 1738, was staying at several addresses in East Yorkshire including North Cave, Welton and Brough.

Here he aspired to the role of country gentleman but to finance this new lifestyle he made frequent excursions into Lincolnshire to commit more crimes. In a sworn statement to three East Riding justices, in October 1738, the publican of the Ferry Inn at Brough, William Harris, claimed that Palmer had lodged with him for four or five months. Harris said that Palmer had made numerous trips into Lincolnshire returning with 'several horses at a time which he sold to diverse persons in the County of York'. The innkeeper told the magistrates that Palmer had claimed that his father and sister lived at Long Sutton but that he had been forced to flee from his father's house because of his debts. These lies were soon to be exposed.

If Turpin's aim, in masquerading as John Palmer, was to keep a low-profile and avoid suspicion then his boastful and bizarre behaviour with Harris and other Brough residents was likely to have the opposite effect. According to the evidence Palmer claimed he had firearms available and that if Harris were to accompany him into Lincolnshire 'twenty pounds is as easily got as two pence'. The testimony of Harris also contained the chilling assertion, which Palmer is said to have made, that 'before they do catch me a great deal of blood shall be spilt'.

However, it was Turpin's erratic and probably drunken antics at Brough on the 2 October 1738 which proved to be decisive. In a statement made on the same day as that of William Harris,

two farm labourers, Abraham Green and John Robinson, claimed that Palmer had, without cause, shot dead 'a tame fowl which did belong to Francis Hall of Brough and did throw the said fowl into the fields of Elloughton'. Furthermore, Robinson complained to the magistrates, that when he tried to remonstrate with Palmer about his unwarranted destruction of someone else's property, Palmer had threatened to shoot him too!

The fact that these witness statements were made on the same day (3 October 1738) suggests some degree of collaboration between Harris, Green and Robinson. If it was Harris who took the lead in bringing Palmer's activities to the notice of the authorities it is not clear what his motive might have been. Harris was the educated one of the three and some years later (in 1749) a record shows that he was also paid to apprehend a Margaret Mitchil and her daughter Susannah and convey them to the Beverley House of Correction.

For the three East Riding magistrates meeting at Beverley on the 3 October 1738 the evidence of Green, Robinson and Harris was enough for them to initiate further action. A warrant for the arrest of John Palmer was issued and, according to legend, he was apprehended at the Green Man Inn in Welton (now the Green Dragon). Questioned by the magistrates Turpin (or Palmer as he was known to them) was not able to provide sureties for his good behaviour

Right: A gamekeeper called Thomas Morris went to Epping Forest on 4 May 1737 to track down Turpin but the highwayman, determined to resist capture, shot Morris dead.

Opposite: Turpin's vicious nature is indicated by this raid at Loughton in Essex. He reputedly held an old widow over an open fire until she agreed to tell them where her valuables were hidden.

and was committed to the Beverley House of Correction while further enquiries took place. Checks made at Long Sutton in Lincolnshire revealed that Palmer had no family at the place as he had claimed and that he had been arrested there on suspicion of sheep stealing but had escaped custody. Faced with the evidence of Palmer's villainy George Crowle, an East Riding JP who had questioned him, ordered that he should be moved from the insecure Beverley House of Correction to York Castle (October 1738). An entry in the County Treasurer's account book held in the East Riding Archives records a payment of £2 2s 0d to 'George Smith and another for conveying John Palmer to York Castle'.

For four months 'Palmer' languished in the cells at York with the authorities unaware that their prisoner was really the infamous highwayman Dick Turpin, wanted in the Home Counties for robbery and murder. The manner in which they discovered his true identity was almost as ludicrous as the circumstances of his arrest in East Yorkshire. To aid his defence Turpin wrote to his brother asking him to obtain character evidence from London 'that would go a great way towards my being acquitted'. Unfortunately for Turpin the letter was intercepted by someone who knew his handwriting despite being written in the name of John Palmer. When it was revealed that Palmer was really Turpin his fate was sealed. The specimen charges against him

The castle at York, *c.* 1750. Turpin was held here (1738-1739) while awaiting trial.

were recorded in a document now held by the National Archives in London. In the indictment of 1 March 1739 against John Palmer, otherwise Richard Turpin, the jurors found him guilty of stealing, at the parish of Welton, a black mare worth three pounds and a filly foal worth twenty shillings. Both horses were the property of Thomas Creasey of Hecklington in Lincolnshire.

In an age when execution was commonly used for a range of crimes, the two charges of horse stealing were enough to warrant the death sentence. In the weeks that followed the trial Turpin achieved a celebrity status and received many visitors in the condemned cell. When facing death he also showed a more generous side to his nature. On the day of his execution, Saturday 7 April 1739, he gave £3 10s 0d to five men who had agreed to act as official mourners and a gold ring to a woman from Brough with whom he had formed a relationship. Determined to make a good show of his final moments Turpin, dressed in new clothes and shoes, was taken by horse-drawn cart from York Castle to the gallows situated on the Tadcaster Road. This was known as the York Tyburn, built like its more famous counterpart in London as a triangular structure with three beams supported by three uprights; locally it was known as the 'three legged mare'.

The public execution attracted a large crowd and they gathered around the gallows to watch Turpin's demise. The grisly job of hangman was performed by Thomas Hadfield, another condemned prisoner, who had been pardoned on condition that he would carry out the execution. A report in the *York Courant* newspaper records that Turpin died bravely: after talking to the executioner for about half-an-hour he threw himself off the ladder and died of strangulation by the noose in about five minutes.

So ended the life and career of one of Britain's most notorious criminals. It seems clear that, in spite of all the romantic stories written about Turpin, the house robber, turned highwayman, turned horse stealer was a menace to a society which had few means to maintain effective law and order. Like so many of his kind, Turpin's undoing was his brash overconfidence. When taking chances before he had always managed to stay one step ahead of the law. However, his reckless behaviour in East Yorkshire, as John Palmer, meant his luck finally ran out.

17

A Giant Celebration: William Bradley of Market Weighton

An important date nowadays in Market Weighton's calendar is Giant Bradley Day. When the celebrations began some years ago they attracted numerous visitors to the town, drawn by the stalls, entertainers and attractions which the day had to offer. The festival was named after Market Weighton's most famous son. William Bradley became, fittingly, the symbol of the same fairground atmosphere that had brought him fame and fortune though not, it has to be said, personal happiness.

The *Guinness Book of Records* states, in its chapter on human dimensions that, throughout history, claims about the height of human beings have often been exaggerated and that stories about giants need to be treated with caution. A wealth of evidence, however, including the *Guinness Book of Records*, suggests that William Bradley of Market Weighton was indeed one such giant. Known as the Yorkshire Giant he stood, by adulthood, at 7ft 9in. tall and weighed 27 stones.

Much of the evidence about Bradley's early life comes to us from information written down in an almanac almost sixty years after his death. Stories handed on by word of mouth are prone to distortion and exaggeration and should therefore be treated with caution. The available evidence suggests that neither of Bradley's parents were tall. In fact there was no reason why they should have been since the growth of the human body is at least partly determined by growth hormone produced by the pituitary gland deep within the brain. It is the overproduction of this hormone, in childhood, which makes a normal-sized human being into a giant. William Bradley was the fourth son of a family of thirteen and was born on the 10 February 1787. At birth he weighed fourteen pounds and by the age of eleven he was eleven stones. Contemporary accounts suggest that in childhood he was tall and slender but that in adolescence he became stout. Although he was the only member of his family to suffer from this abnormality he did have a sister who, had she lived, might have been just as tall. Unfortunately she died in an accident at the age of sixteen.

It is likely that Bradley's size and weight set him apart from other children from early in his life and made him the butt of their insults and cruel humour, even if they were also afraid of him. The oral evidence passed down to us from the early nineteenth century suggests that the mockery he suffered made him feel unhappy, isolated and melancholy and that he bore a 'vacant look'. Bradley is said to have attended Joseph Mosey's school in Market Weighton; anecdotal evidence suggests that the schoolmaster used Bradley's height to punish other boys by lifting

Left: William Bradley, the 'Yorkshire Giant', from a contemporary engraving.

Opposite: 'Marvels of nature' like Giant Bradley were the stock-in-trade of travelling fairs in the nineteenth century.

them up and leaving them to cling to the roof beams. Further evidence suggests that Bradley was already ill-at-ease with his fame as a giant and was resentful of the curiosity of others. The story is told of two gentlemen who came to see him at school and who asked him to stand up from his desk so that they could judge his height for themselves. Bradley, it is said, obstinately refused their requests despite being offered a bribe to do so! Feeding and clothing such a child must have been an expensive business for his parents; it has been claimed that his appetite was so huge that, by himself, he could eat a large leg of mutton with ease.

Schooling at the end of the eighteenth century was designed to equip a child with the basics of reading, writing and arithmetic but little else. Furthermore, since education at this time was not free it seems that Bradley's parents must have been pleased when their son was old enough to leave school and start work as a farm labourer in the Pocklington area to supplement the family income. However, at a time when the average wage of a farm labourer was less than 10 shillings the prospect of promoting their giant son as a fairground attraction must have seemed attractive to them. In an age before fairground rides the exhibition of freaks, monstrosities and 'marvels of nature' were an important part of most travelling shows. At the beginning of the nineteenth century the dwarfs, tall men, bearded ladies, Siamese twins and so on, were a marketable product for a curious public. The fairground showman was a vital part of the act and it was his skill at story-telling and presentation which could transform a person with physical abnormalities into a successful sideshow exhibit. Freak shows involving giants, however distasteful they might seem to us day, were the stock-in-trade of travelling fairs, shop front exhibitions and markets. Other nineteenth-century exhibits included Sam Taylor, the Ilkeston Giant; Patrick O'Brien, the Irish Giant and William Bradley, the Yorkshire Giant. The name of the showman who took control of Giant Bradley's life at this time has not been recorded but there seems little doubt that promises of fame and fortune were made

to both William Bradley and his father to lure him into the life of the fairground attraction. The size and stature of William Bradley as Britain's tallest man made him into a valuable and sensational commodity and he was exhibited with another wonder of the age, a monster pig, 'The Yorkshire Pig', bred at the nearby village of Sancton. Fairs like the famous Hull Fair and Nottingham Goose Fair were common in the early nineteenth century and it is likely that Bradley's fame grew as he travelled by horse drawn caravan to towns and villages all over England.

It is recorded that at some point in his show career Bradley and his minder parted company when he discovered that the showman was defrauding him. Whatever the truth of this accusation Bradley now began to exhibit himself privately in rooms he hired in various towns and by 1815 was charging one shilling for admission. This would have provided him with far more than he could ever have hoped to earn as a farm labourer in Market Weighton. A handbill which survives from the Hull Fair of 1815 (then held in the Old Town) records that William Bradley could be seen at 15 Queen Street and would fill spectators with 'wonder and astonishment'. In an age when royal patronage was considered to be an important marketing tool Bradley also made use, in his advertising, of the fact that he had been granted an audience with 'their Majesties and Royal Family at Windsor'. One of the possessions that Bradley treasured until his death was a gold watch, presented to him by King George III.

After years of travelling from town to town in caravans and living cooped up in cramped conditions Bradley's health began to decline and he returned to Market Weighton. He could now afford to live the life of a gentleman rather than a farm labourer and resided at a house in Northgate (now 89 York Road). This had been specially built to accommodate his height and bulk. These latter years were spent in ill-health and seclusion. According to reports he went lame and had to support his great bulk with a crutch nearly 7ft in length. The years of being

William Bradley's house in York Road, Market Weighton.

an object of curiosity had also taken its toll on him mentally and henceforth Bradley jealously guarded his privacy; he lived the life of a recluse often hiding if people came near. Neither could the wealth he had acquired protect him from illness in an age when doctors had few answers to sickness; in 1820 Bradley contracted tuberculosis (TB). In 1820 the germ theory of disease did not yet exist and would not do so until 1861 when Louis Pasteur published his findings on the subject. It would require further research into TB bacteria by the German scientist Robert Koch in the late nineteenth century and the development of powerful drugs like penicillin in the twentieth century before a deadly disease like tuberculosis could be dealt with. For a man like William Bradley living long before any of this there was no hope of a cure and he died on the 30 May 1820 aged only thirty-three years. Even at the end it seems that the press of the time could not avoid exaggeration; the *Hull Advertiser* recorded his death in its edition of 2 June 1820 in the following way: 'On Wednesday at Market Weighton, Mr Bradley, the Yorkshire Giant who measured 9 feet in length and 3 feet across the shoulders'.

It was likely that the funeral of such a noted local celebrity would provoke curiosity and Bradley had sought to prevent this by asking for an early morning burial. However, even though his funeral was held at 5am on 3 June 1820 the timing did not prevent a large crowd from gathering to watch the huge coffin being lowered into the grave at All Saints church, Market Weighton. Fears that grave robbers might not leave him in peace led to the later exhumation of the body and re-interment inside the church itself.

Although local people may have been anxious to protect Bradley's corpse from being sold to some foreign museum or collector of anatomical curiosities, many sought to collect their own souvenirs of the great man. Bradley's shoes, inner soles, and stockings are just some of the items which went into the collections of local residents. As a reminder of Bradley himself there is his house in York Road and the memorial to him in Market Weighton church. There are also plans to build a life size statue of him although the original plan to make it from bronze may turn out to be too expensive an option!

18

Carling: The World Class Beer with the East Yorkshire Connection

According to a recent claim Britain's biggest selling lager is the Carling brand with over five million barrels sold each year across the nation's pubs and clubs. The Carling story has quite modest origins and its beginnings were in the small East Yorkshire village of Etton.

The county of Yorkshire has a great tradition of brewing beer and famous names such as Joshua Tetley and John Smith have long associations with places like Leeds and Tadcaster. However, the name of Thomas Carling and the village of Etton might be less familiar to most people. Even today Etton is a quiet picturesque place nestling amid the rolling hills of the Yorkshire Wolds close to the town of Beverley. In the year of Thomas Carling's birth, 1797, it was quieter still with just a few scattered farmhouses and cottages and three large open fields, communally farmed with arable strips, and common grazing land to the west of the village. Thomas Carling's baptism record from Etton church records that his father, William Carling, was a farm labourer, although by 1823 a local directory described him as a farmer. In those days East Riding villages like Etton were far more self-sufficient than they are today. The same 1823 directory lists a number of trades to serve local needs at a time when rural transport was still slow and difficult. These trades included a boot and shoemaker, a tailor, a corn miller and two shopkeepers. The production of beer was also very much a cottage industry and we know that William Carling brewed his own.

In the early nineteenth century Etton, like many other English villages, was undergoing profound changes. In order to improve farming efficiency the scattered strips were being gathered together in enclosed farms. The Etton Enclosure Act was passed in 1818 and this may explain William Carling's change of status from farm labourer to farmer. It may also help to explain why, in 1818, his twenty-year old son, Thomas, (the youngest of William's five children) decided to leave Etton and seek his fortune in Canada.

The nineteenth century was a time when many working-class people, seeking a better life and the chance to own land of their own, left for the colonies. Without a friend or acquaintance aboard the ship, Thomas Carling sailed from Hull on 17 May 1818. Arriving in Quebec a month later he then began an arduous journey on foot and by boat to London Township in Ontario where he obtained rights to one hundred acres of land. By the end of 1819 Carling was clearing trees to create farmland, building a log cabin and within a year had married the daughter of another pioneering family: Margaret Routledge. They brought up five children together in an area of Canada that was still largely wilderness, far from any settlement, with the discomfort of

Thomas Carling of Etton, East Yorkshire and London Township, Ontario, Canada.

hard winters and danger from wild animals. On one occasion as Thomas Carling returned home through the woods he was attacked by a large wolf. Armed only with a walking stick he managed to kill it after a desperate fight. As one of the earliest settlers in this area of Canada Thomas Carling would have needed even greater self-reliance than he would have done had he stayed in East Yorkshire, for there were few other tradesmen. Years later his son, John Carling, explained 'until I was ten I never wore a shoe on my foot or a coat on my back that was not made by my father or my mother'. John Carling remarked that although his father knew nothing about shoemaking, necessity forced him to learn, for his sons needed footwear as they grew up:

> He would make his own lasts and then he would kill a young animal and take the skin to the tannery (Delaware). The tanner would keep half the hides for his pay. In this way my father used to make all our shoes.

After twenty years of enduring the hardships of Ontario farm life Thomas Carling sold his land and moved his family to the nearby settlement of London Township. In 1839, when looking

Above: The Carling Brewery in London Township, Ontario opened in 1878.

Right: Sir John Carling (son of Thomas Carling), brewer and politician, seen here with his granddaughter in about 1905.

for something new to occupy his time, his thoughts turned to the home-brewed beer that his father had made back in East Yorkshire. It was now that fate came to his aid. There was a large British garrison stationed in London Township and its troops were entitled to six pints of beer a day. Impressed by the quality of Carling's Yorkshire-inspired beer the officers and men persuaded him to start brewing it commercially in 1840. The brewery used a single horse, walking round and round to turn the mill that ground the malt and it employed six strong men to work the mash tubs.

Around 1849 Thomas Carling's sons William and John took over the brewery in Waterloo Street while their father, weakened in later years by heart problems, slipped into retirement. He died in February 1880, aged 82.

Under the stewardship of Thomas Carling's sons the business continued to prosper. By 1860 the Carling brand was so successful that the brewery was buying over 18,000 bushels of grain each year, over 12,000 pounds of hops and horse power had been replaced by steam power. This success helped to fund the political career of John Carling who went on to become a member of the Ontario legislature and Federal Agriculture Minister 1885-1892. For his long service to Canadian politics John Carling was knighted by Queen Victoria in 1893.

In 1878 the Carling brothers abandoned the old brewery and moved to a new purpose built one, costing a quarter of a million dollars. Although this was badly damaged in a fire during 1879 John Carling showed his skill as a businessman by restarting production ten weeks later. By 1890 Carling's workforce of 100 men was turning out over 30,000 barrels of ale and porter each year and also producing lager.

Despite other problems in later years, like the introduction of prohibition in the USA (1920-1933), the Carling brewing business continued to grow. New products were developed (the Carling Black Label brand was first brewed in Canada in 1926) and although the business passed out of the hands of the Carling family in the 1930s the name lives on. Today Carling is a global brand made by many different brewers around the world including Coors in the United Kingdom. The world-leading Carling brand name is therefore a fitting tribute to the Yorkshire emigrant, Thomas Carling, who took his father's brewing skills to the New World and made them into a commercial success.

19

When Darkest Africa Came To East Yorkshire: The Brandesburton Pygmies

One hundred years ago the residents of Brandesburton, in rural East Yorkshire, were astonished to learn of some new arrivals in their village. For centuries there had been a fascination, in western cultures at least, with small human beings. Stories like *Gulliver's Travels* fed this interest and explorers had continued to search for legendary lost tribes of diminutive human beings, well into the nineteenth century. When publications about newly discovered equatorial Africa showed that diminutive people really did exist, there were some individuals who were ready to exploit this situation among a curious public.

The grounds of Brandesburton Hall in East Yorkshire might seem a bizarre home for a group of African pygmies and yet from 1905 to 1907 six of them could be seen there, at various times, hunting small game with bows and arrows. How they came to be there is testament to the kind of greed and exploitation that sometimes characterised Europe's relationship with Africa in the nineteenth and early twentieth century.

The pygmies, at about four and a half feet tall, are the smallest people in Africa. Another characteristic which set them apart from other Africans was that they did not plant gardens, or work iron or make pottery preferring the life of hunter-gatherers in the tropical forests of modern-day Zaire (then the Belgian Congo). It was here, in 1904, that they came to the attention of a big-game hunter, Colonel James Harrison of Brandesburton Hall. Harrison, like other members of the East Riding gentry, enjoyed a privileged background and as a young man progressed from Harrow and Oxford to a career in the Army. His army career and his frequent hunting trips to Abyssinia, Uganda and the Congo between 1885 and 1904 must have been a drain on the Harrison family fortune which may explain his interest in the African pygmies. His diary, for 4 March 1904, records his first encounter with them in a typically condescending style: 'Saw my first pygmy man – quite a quaint looking object'.

Although Harrison was later to claim that he brought six of the Ituri Forest pygmies to England to satisfy the curiosity of his friends, there seems little doubt that he also saw the commercial possibilities of exhibiting them in theatres and music halls all over the country. Before going back to the Congo he had already entered into a contract with the Moss-Stoll Empire Theatre Circuit (owners of the London Hippodrome) to exhibit a group of pygmies with them. Although Harrison was to claim that the six 'little people' he brought to London in June 1905 were volunteers, when questioned by Foreign Office officials it was said that they would prefer to return to their forests. Despite disapproval of the whole enterprise by the British

Above: Colonel Harrison with the Ituri Forest pygmies *en route* to Britain. (courtesy Beverley Local Studies Library)

Left: Studio photograph of the Pygmies as they appeared on stage. Back row, left to right: Bokane (chief), Matuka. Front row: Kuarke (Princess), Mongonga, Mafutiminga, Amuriape.

Opposite: Another of Harrison's marketing ploys was the release of five phonograph records of the pygmies by the Gramophone Company in the spring of 1906. (courtesy Beverley Local Studies Library)

Foreign Secretary, Lord Lansdowne, the pygmies were allowed into Britain. The controversy surrounding their arrival led to criticism of Harrison who was described, in some quarters, as an 'aggressive controversialist' and, more sarcastically, as the 'dwarf impresario'.

For Harrison the controversy secured free publicity for his stage act; he told a reporter that 'thousands will be glad of a chance of seeing what they have read so much about'. In his publicity statements Harrison carefully constructed an image of the pygmies as 'savages' for maximum effect. It would seem that Harrison needed all the press interest he could get in his pygmies for the performances of the six were hardly stimulating. The four male and two female pygmies appeared on stage against a background of a tropical forest armed with spears, bows and arrows. To the beat of a drum one of the Africans would begin a chant, the other males would dance while both the females remained seated. During their first appearance, on 5 June 1905 at the London Hippodrome, the applause of the audience so startled them that they stopped performing altogether! When they appeared at the Manchester Hippodrome in October 1905 a local newspaper described them as 'interesting as curiosities but disappointing as entertainers' while their feeble attempts to hide their faces from the audience led to hoots of derision from the occupants of the cheaper seats in the gallery.

The arrival of the pygmies in East Yorkshire on 28 July 1905 caused great excitement and Harrison hired a bus to take them from Beverley railway station to his home at Brandesburton Hall. A few days later, on a Bank Holiday Monday, Harrison put them on display at the Hall to a paying audience of three thousand people many of whom had cycled there to witness the event. A week later they were at Londesborough Park, near Market Weighton where hundreds saw them dance. To further entertain the crowd the pygmies displayed their hunting skills with bows, arrows and spears when rabbits were released from sacks for the purpose. The event was so successful that their host, Lord Londesborough, welcomed them back for a second visit on 27 August 1905. Under Harrison's guidance the pygmies also appeared on stage at York, Hull, Scarborough, Bridlington, Withernsea, Hornsea and Driffield.

There is little doubt that Harrison used every means available to cash in on the curiosity value of the pygmies. When they appeared at the Beverley Assembly Rooms in October 1905, for example, reserved seats cost 1s 6d, a considerable sum by early twentieth-century standards. Another of Harrison's marketing ploys was the release of five phonograph records of the pygmies by the Gramophone Company in the spring of 1906.

Between performances that took them all over England (there was also a visit to Berlin) the pygmies were allowed to roam free in the grounds at Brandesburton Hall, building shelters and hunting birds and rabbits. They were a familiar sight at the Brandesburton Forge where the village blacksmith watched them turn horseshoe nails into arrowheads.

It seems likely that the health of the pygmies suffered as a result of their exposure to the English climate; three of them caught pneumonia during the chill winter of 1905. During her stay one of the pygmy women, Princess Amuriape, gave birth to a child, apparently stillborn. Perhaps reflecting her superstitious nature she is reported to have said: 'no child of hers should be born in an alien land'. Although Harrison could be accused of exploiting the pygmies for his own financial gain there is no evidence that he deliberately neglected their health. He employed nurses when they were ill and even paid for a large summerhouse to be added to Brandesburton Hall to create a hot humid atmosphere for his guests.

The pygmies remained in Britain for two years giving their final 'performance' in Hull in November 1907. Harrison then returned them to their forest homeland. It was reported by one Brandesburton resident that 'exhibiting the pygmies was not the financial success that Squire Harrison hoped it would be'.

Whether the pygmies wished to stay so long is not recorded; some claimed they were unhappy and bored while the Aborigines Protection Society condemned the theatrical exploitation of a shy, childlike people. However, the evidence suggests that the pygmies could not be compelled to do things they did not want to do. One of the people engaged by Harrison to look after the pygmies during their theatrical tours, William Hoffman, remarked that occasionally they would not cooperate: 'refusing to perform, sitting on their little chairs and grimacing broadly and nothing I could do would make them alter their minds'.

20

Lease of Life: When Ealing Studios came to East Yorkshire

The varied and often spectacular landscapes of Yorkshire have long been a favourite of film and television producers seeking to find attractive locations for their work. The BBC drama series *All Creatures Great and Small*, the Ken Loach movie *Kes* and the Yorkshire Television series *Heartbeat* are all good examples of this. An earlier pioneer of the Yorkshire location for filming was Ealing Studios. In the late 1940s and early 1950s Ealing was in the forefront of Britain's film industry with such classic comedies as *Kind Hearts and Coronets*, *Passport to Pimlico* and the *Lavender Hill Mob*. In early 1954 the Ealing production team, led by Sir Michael Balcon, had a new project in hand called *Lease of Life*. The story concerned a Yorkshire vicar given twelve months to live and the effect this had on his faith and his family. During March and April 1954 the making of the film was to bring the famous actor Robert Donat and an Ealing production team to the beautiful East Yorkshire village of Lund and the Gothic splendours of Beverley Minster.

Although Ealing Studios were best known for their comedy output they also had a flair for serious drama that reflected the British way of life. The film *Lease of Life*, based on a story by Frank Baker, concerned an impoverished, middle-aged country clergyman called William Thorne, the vicar of the village of Hinton St John, who discovered that he only had a year to live. In the story Thorne was invited to give a sermon on School Founders Day at the local cathedral of Gilchester and, inspired by thoughts of his imminent demise, he decided to throw caution to the wind and deliver a highly controversial sermon to the congregation.

In late 1953 and early 1954 the production team of the new film (provisionally called 'The West Window') was searching for locations for the fictional town of Gilchester and the village of Hinton St John. They were looking for a cathedral-type church which would not be confused with Canterbury or York. One of the Ealing staff was the son of the then Archbishop of Canterbury, Geoffrey Fisher. Taking a keen interest in the project, the Archbishop suggested that Beverley Minster would be a suitable location for Gilchester Cathedral. Meanwhile the nearby Wolds village of Lund became the setting for Thorne's own parish of Hinton St John. The real vicar of Lund, the Revd Lancelot Foster, recorded how, on the 21 January 1954, men from Ealing Studios arrived to take photographs of the church and the vicarage. When Foster asked if they had permission to take photographs he was told that approval had been given by higher authorities! Ever mindful of good public relations the producers invited the vicar's wife to Ealing in March 1954 to see the replicas of her kitchen, hall and lounge that they had built in the studio.

A significant number of the best names in Britain's film industry at that time were involved in

Theatre and film actor Robert Donat is seen here performing the lead role of Revd William Thorne, in *Lease of Life*, on location in Lund with director Charles Frend, 1954. (courtesy *Hull Daily Mail* and East Riding Archives Service)

the making of *Lease of Life*. The director, Charles Frend, had worked with Alfred Hitchcock and his previous films included *Scott of the Antarctic* (1948) and *The Cruel Sea* (1953). Frend's love of the English countryside was reflected in the masterly skills of the film's cinematographer, Douglas Slocombe, who made excellent use of Eastmancolour photography to capture the beauty of the East Yorkshire Wolds. Slocombe's career spanned over forty years and his photography was later rewarded with Oscar-nominations, BAFTAs and a Lifetime Achievement Award in 1995.

The story and the setting for *Lease of Life* called for a bleak wintry outlook and so the location shooting at Lund began on the 21 March 1954. Film stars, production staff and technicians with cameras, arc lights and miles of electric cable descended on the little community and the village hall became their canteen. The producers had already been recruiting local talent in Beverley and surrounding villages for smaller parts and to be 'extras'. On 20 March, Robert Newton an assistant producer at Ealing, had been in Beverley to watch the St Nicholas Players in a J.M. Barrie play called *Half an Hour.* Although it is not recorded if any of the amateurs were given roles in the forthcoming film, we do know that ladies from Lockington, Lund, Walkington and Dalton Holme did have parts.

The filming provided both momentary fame and some paid employment to Lund residents.

Director, Charles Frend and his assistant carry the script of *Lease of Life* written by Eric Ambler. Note the camera track lying along the pavement and the film lighting needed for filming on dark winter days. (courtesy of *Hull Daily Mail* and East Riding Archives Service)

We are told that Farmer Walker received thirty shillings for going to church and that his son got two guineas for riding a bike down the main street. David Freear, Lund resident and retired postman, was required by the director to sit reading a newspaper but to look astonished as well!

Newspaper accounts from the time also give us a fascinating insight into how village life has changed in the intervening fifty years. Some of the filming took place at the village green where blacksmith Alfred Teal 'continued working at his forge despite the fact that spotlights were focused just outside'. Mr Teal told a reporter that he had never seen a film in his life and was unsure whether he would make the trip into Beverley to see this one when it was released! The director also made use of Mr Wharram's tailor's shop, which became a tobacconist's for the purpose of the film. Today, the village of Lund has neither blacksmith nor shop.

The location shooting brought a host of actors and actresses to Lund and Beverley, many of them household names. In the lead role of the Revd William Thorne was the outstanding theatre and film actor Robert Donat, star of Alfred Hitchcock's *The 39 Steps* (1935) and *Goodbye Mr Chips* (1939). *Lease of Life* was Donat's penultimate film appearance and the sad irony of his performance was that he was a dying man playing a dying man. Donat suffered from asthma

Left: Studio portrait of Robert Donat, 1930s.

Below: The former blacksmith's workshop of Alfred Teal who 'continued working at his forge despite the spotlights focused just outside'.

and such was the fragile nature of his health that oxygen cylinders were kept close by when he was acting. In some scenes from *Lease of Life* Donat's breathless delivery of his lines is a clear indication of the health problems that were to end his life four years later. Despite these difficulties Donat gave one of his greatest performances as the dying vicar and was nominated best actor for this role at the 8th British Film Academy Awards.

Playing the part of Thorne's wife Vera was Kay Walsh who starred in over sixty films between 1934 and 1981. This accomplished actress gave audiences a fine performance as a poverty-stricken spouse trapped in a remote country parish and obsessed by the need to get her musically-gifted daughter through music college. This latter role (Susan Thorne) went to the young Scottish actress Adrienne Corri who was later to feature in Stanley Kubrick's controversial film *Clockwork Orange*. Taking the part of Susan's piano teacher, Martin Blake, was a gifted young British actor called Denholm Elliott. His film career had begun in 1949 and in the 1950s he tended to play pleasant but ineffectual characters. Denholm Elliott went on to act in over 100 films and his later career included the part of Marcus Brody in *Raiders of the Lost Ark* (1981) and *Indiana Jones and the Last Crusade* (1989). Sadly, Elliott's still thriving career was cut short in 1992 when died of complications brought on by AIDS.

Apart from the usual difficulties of location filming far from the studio the work at Lund was also put at risk by an industrial dispute in London. Film-laboratory technicians there went on strike with the result that the Lund cameramen could not see rushes of their work and check whether they needed to be re-shot. To make sure, some scenes were filmed six times because as the director, Charles Frend, told local reporters it would be impossible to return to Lund to do them again.

At the beginning of April the Ealing unit moved to Beverley for scenes in the market place and at 'Gilchester Cathedral'. The Minster became an outsize studio with craftsmen installing an altar and a bigger pulpit for the filming of Thorne's sermon. Since these scenes represented a School Founder's Day service, pupils were drafted in from Beverley Grammar School to provide the schoolboy congregation. The arrival of such a celebrated group of people was, of course, a major social event in 1950s Beverley and the stars and the production team were invited to a civic reception at the Hall in Lairgate on 3 April 1954.

The film *Lease of Life* received its London premiere in October 1954 but local people had to wait until January 1955 before it received its first screening in Beverley (at the Playhouse). Opinions about the film itself remain mixed. It is perhaps an indication of the film's minority appeal, or perhaps its sombre story line, that it is seen so rarely today. Compared to Ealing's more lighter film offerings *Lease of Life* has failed to stand the test of time, even though some of its themes are as relevant today as they were in the 1950s (eg. decline in church attendance, tabloid journalism). Furthermore, as well as giving us a commanding performance by the actor Robert Donat in one of his last films, the colour cinematography of Douglas Slocombe perfectly captures the atmospheric charm of the Yorkshire Wolds some fifty years ago.

21

Radio 270: When A Pirate Ruled The Yorkshire Airwaves

With the advent of digital technology today's listeners can enjoy a multitude of radio programmes catering for every conceivable taste in sound broadcasting. A host of BBC and commercial channels compete to provide the radio audience with an unprecedented choice of local and national output. As commonplace as this seems today, the BBC sound broadcasting monopoly was only effectively broken in the 1960s by the determined efforts of a few offshore radio pioneers.

Beginning in the 1920s the history of radio in the United Kingdom was dominated by the government's attempts to keep this powerful new medium under their control. In 1927 the British Broadcasting Corporation was created, paid for by charging listeners a licence fee. The BBC wireless service, by broadcasting speeches, lectures and educational material, often reflecting the high-brow intellectual tastes of its creators rather than more popular styles of programming. Increasingly the British population turned to British overseas programmes broadcast by continental stations such as Radio Normandy and, above all, Radio Luxembourg. Despite the efforts of the British government to discourage rivals to the BBC, by 1938 Radio Luxembourg had 45% of the Sunday listening audience compared to the BBC's 35%.

After the Second World War the BBC's radio monopoly continued while Radio Luxembourg's medium wave transmitter, often marred by fading and atmospheric interference, broadcast commercial programmes to the UK in the evenings. The output of Radio Luxembourg was dominated the big record companies like Decca and Parlophone and it was difficult for new artists to get air time for their work. To break this stranglehold an Irish businessman called Ronan O'Rahilly purchased an old ferry vessel and converted it into a sea-borne transmitting studio. On Easter Sunday 1964 this vessel became Britain's first offshore radio station; Radio Caroline.

Caroline helped to inspire a host of imitators including Yorkshire's own offshore station: Radio 270. This was the brainchild of Don Robinson, a Scarborough-based entrepreneur and pop promoter who had met Ronan O'Rahilly and was impressed by the success of Radio Caroline. In November 1965, Robinson called a meeting with Bill Pashby, a fishing boat owner and Roland Hill, a local farmer. Together with industrialist Leonard Dale and local supermarket tycoon, Wilf Proudfoot (who became managing director of the station) enthusiasm for the offshore radio project gathered pace although potential investors were warned that the enterprise was 'high risk'.

Above left: Radio 270 proved to be a tourist attraction and cruises to the ship (moored three miles out in international waters) proved to be popular. (courtesy www.offshore-radio.de)

Above right: Radio 270 car stickers helped publicise the station.

The new company purchased an old Dutch herring drifter for £2,500 (*Oceaan 7*) from a port near the Hague and this sailed to Guernsey for the fitting of a 154ft high antenna costing £10,000. Work then began, in early 1966, to fit out the ship with studio equipment, generators and a transmitter. At only 118ft long, the vessel was small but initially this was not considered a problem since the original idea was to tape the shows onshore for broadcasting later. It was only when the plans were changed to include live broadcasts that the cramped limitations of the *Oceaan 7* became a problem. The ship's fish hold, for example, was turned into very spartan living accommodation.

The new station was due to begin broadcasting beyond territorial limits, off Scarborough, on the 1 April 1966. However, the launch was delayed by the late arrival of transmitter parts from the USA, much to the embarrassment of the company who had invited shareholders and the press to Scarborough's Grand Hotel to hear the first broadcast. Worse was to follow. The next day a force-7 gale brought the transmitting mast crashing down and £10,000 of the company's money disappeared under the waters of the North Sea. Several more weeks were then lost while repairs were carried out in Grimsby before the ship was able to return to her Scarborough anchorage and begin broadcasting test transmissions on 7 June 1966. The first record played was Frank Sinatra's 'Strangers in the Night'. The official launch of the station took place on Saturday 11 June 1966.

Presenter Hal Yorke in the Radio 270 studio.

Further difficulties were to follow including questions in a national newspaper about the ship's seaworthiness. Despite the technical glitches which were to plague Radio 270 during its relatively short operational life, June 1966 to August 1967, there is little doubt that it provided a popular alternative to the old-fashioned output of the BBC's Light Programme. Those who tuned in on their transistor radios to 269 metres medium wave were offered a type of programming unknown to Yorkshire radio up to that point. Radio 270 offered continuous and up-to-date pop music (with original records rather than cover versions), American-style jingles, commercials and the informal banter of a new generation of disc-jockeys. By Christmas 1966 Radio 270 had adopted the more dynamic style of American radio stations (like Radio WABC New York) with a 'Top Forty' format and this continued until the station closed.

One of Radio 270's disc jockeys, Paul Burnett, had already worked on British Forces Radio in Aden and after the closure of Radio 270 he went on to develop a successful career with Manx Radio, Radio Luxembourg and BBC's Radio One. His experience as a broadcaster on the high seas was not always pleasant as he suffered badly from seasickness, an occupational hazard of working on Radio 270. Another of the station's memorable broadcasters was Peter 'Boots' Bowman who had already worked on another offshore station, Radio Scotland, before joining Radio 270. Meanwhile, today's viewers, who regularly tune into the BBC's News 24 television channel, will have seen the veteran newsreader Phillip Hayton. He too began his broadcasting career in the North Sea aboard *Oceaan 7* and in rough weather his ability to withstand seasickness meant that he had to carry on broadcasting while his less robust colleagues lay indisposed!

The Radio 270 disc jockeys were paid £25 a week, working three weeks out of every four. After two weeks broadcasting on board *Oceaan 7*, their third week was spent ashore selling commercials at two or three pounds a time. To encourage those Yorkshire businesses that were suspicious of the new medium, they were given free advertising slots to encourage them to buy more. In the East Riding these advertisers included Hull's 'Sydney Scarborough' record shop, eager to cash in on the popularity of Radio 270 among a growing teenage audience.

To raise further revenue the station also advertised its own products, like transistor radios and electric sanders, direct to the public and organized pop concerts at places like the Spa in Bridlington. The company's balance sheet also benefited from a payment of £800 each week from the American 'Church of God'. The station, like many others, broadcast the sermons of the evangelist Garner Ted Armstrong in his programme called 'The World Tomorrow'.

By June 1967 a National Opinion Poll estimated that Radio 270 had captured 4.75 million listeners stretching from Newcastle to the East Midlands. However, the days of the station were numbered because of the determination of Harold Wilson's Labour Government to close down all the offshore radio stations. Despite the popularity of broadcasters like Radio 270, Radio London and Radio Caroline protestors were told that the pirates were illegally using frequencies which did not belong to them, caused interference to legitimate broadcasters and that these activities had even led to deaths. Despite overwhelming public support for their cause the offshore stations campaigned in vain against the Marine Broadcast Offences Bill that made its way through Parliament through the spring and summer of 1967.

In order to comply with the new law, destined to take effect from 15 August 1967, Radio 270 announced that it would cease transmissions shortly before midnight on 14 August. A final show was planned in which all the presenters would say their farewells but in the event bad weather prevented many from reaching the ship. It was therefore arranged, unofficially, for a helicopter on a training flight from RAF Leconfield to fly taped messages out to the vessel anchored in international waters off Bridlington. Unfortunately, the package missed its intended target and fell into the sea. When it became known that a RAF helicopter had been used for this unauthorised activity an angry Prime Minister, Harold Wilson, ordered an enquiry and the crew received a reprimand!

So ended 430 days of broadcasting by Yorkshire's own offshore radio station, sunk by the Marine Broadcasting Offences Act. With the Radio 270 presenters gone, *Oceaan 7* sailed for Whitby where the broadcasting equipment was removed while the ship itself was eventually scrapped. Although, in the short term, the offshore stations lost their fight to stay on air their presence did have important long-term effects, not least in showing that there was public demand for local, commercial radio. In a real sense Yorkshire's commercial stations of today, like Radio Aire and Viking Radio, owe their existence, in part, to the efforts of those pioneers who braved the North Sea in the late sixties.

22

Fighting Crime: Rough Justice In East Yorkshire

One of Beverley's heritage sites, the Sessions House in New Walk, has undergone a makeover in order to transform it from a centre of justice into a day spa. When first opened in the early nineteenth century the East Riding Sessions House and the adjoining House of Correction provided an important new facility for dealing with wrong-doers.

The elegant Sessions House in Beverley's New Walk, built between 1805-1810, was not the first building in the town where justice was dispensed. In the seventeenth century a building at Hall Garth (south of Beverley Minster) was used and in the eighteenth century part of Beverley's Guildhall became the Sessions House. The Justices also rented a section of the Guildhall as a prison or House of Correction. The name 'House of Correction' suggests that there was in the minds of those interested in penal systems a desire to reform as well as punish However, attempts to find an answer to the problem of reform of offenders were not begun in earnest until much later.

A prisoner in Beverley's House of Correction in the eighteenth century was likely to be there either awaiting trial or awaiting the punishment which the court had given. A report of 1805 records that this prison accommodation had three sleeping cells on the ground floor, four cells on the upper floors (each about nine feet by six feet) and that the East Riding Justices allowed the inmates 'straw on plank bedsteads and five chaldrons of coal yearly'. This same report records that when an inspection took place, on 25 August 1802, there were only six prisoners: one felon and five for petty offences. An examination of the records of the East Riding Quarter Sessions helps to show that this House of Correction was a place to confine prisoners until trial or sentence rather that as a punishment in its own right. The punishments handed out by the justices of the time could, by our standards, seem very harsh indeed. For example, in 1800, a labourer called John Bainton from Cottingham stood accused that on the 9 March he had obtained one guinea by 'false pretences with an intent to cheat and defraud Frances Mackintosh'. Found guilty by the East Riding jury he was ordered to be confined in the House of Correction until the next day at noon and then to be taken to Cottingham and there 'to be publicly whipped for 100 yards'. The pillory, whipping, fines and transportation to the colonies were the kinds of punishment handed out for crimes, which today, seem trivial. One might sympathise, for example, with people like Robert Brisk of Burstwick who in 1740 was sentenced to be transported for seven years for stealing two rings or with Margaret Boulton of Yapham who was publicly whipped at Pocklington for stealing wedding clothes in 1743. Similarly, in 1808, Robert Eskritt, a farm

An engraving of the Beverley Sessions House, *c.* 1830. To the rear of this building was the Beverley House of Correction. (courtesy Beverley Local Studies Library)

Nos 5 to 7 Norfolk Street, Beverley, formerly housed the treadmill of the Beverley House of Correction. Nos 11 to 13 Norfolk Street were once the men's prison cells. Cut into the brickwork of these houses are reminders of the cruelty of the treadmill. One inscription reads 'Oh, my poor leg' and there are calendars used by inmates to mark off their sentences, day-by-day.

A treadmill of the type used at the Beverley House of Correction for hard labour.

labourer of Garton on the Wolds, was found guilty of extortion and sentenced to stand in the Driffield pillory on three consecutive market days.

During the early nineteenth century reform of the criminal law meant a reduction in the number of hanging offences. Although transportation to Australia remained an attractive option to the courts there was a need to expand prisons too. When Beverley's new House Of Correction was opened off New Walk in 1810 it only contained 22 cells but further building work added to this number giving, by 1835, a total of 126 cells. This increase was necessary to allow the introduction of a fashionable new way of dealing with prisoners introduced from the USA: the Silent System. Rules and Regulations of the New Walk prison, published in 1835, stated that 'no prisoner shall, under any pretence, speak or hold any other communication with any other prisoner without special leave'. The aim of the rule on keeping silence was to stop prisoners exchanging evil thoughts and corrupting each other. At Beverley a breach of this rule could be punished by depriving the prisoner of his or her supper or with solitary confinement for up to three days. To detect a breach of the regulation the Keeper of the House could appoint trusted prisoners as wardsmen, or wardswomen, to inform on those who broke the silence rule. To make the job attractive these trusted prisoners were given extra rations of half-a-pound of bread and five ounces of boiled beef a day to supplement the meagre prison diet of bread and oatmeal porridge.

Another major aim of the Silent System was to make prison life so tough that a criminal would be frightened into reforming his or her behaviour and, on release, become worthy citizens. With this aim in mind the prisoners were expected to perform hard labour on the treadmill that had been installed in 1823. At Beverley the power of human muscles on this 'everlasting staircase' was used to work machinery which produced whiting from chalk: the treadmill was a cylinder with steps around its circumference and the prisoners had to climb from step to step and keep it moving for up to 20 minutes at a time. It has been estimated that by the end of this period they would have ascended 1,100 steps. After ten minutes rest the ordeal would then begin again until they had completed their allotted 'labour of ascent'. The rules of 1835 stated that the work performed by prisoners on the treadmill should not exceed 12,000ft per day for men and 10,000ft per day for women; such a marathon task would, of course, have required many periods of 20 minutes in a single day. Prisoners on the treadmill were separated from each other by a wooden screen to prevent talking.

Two of the prisoners who would probably have worked the treadmill were William Rogers and John Hall; in October 1836 they were sentenced to fourteen days with hard labour for stealing apples from the garden of Richard Jameson of Beverley. A further entry from the records of the East Riding Quarter Sessions, from 1844, shows the conviction of the prostitute Catherine O'Brien of Liverpool for being a rogue and a vagabond in that she did 'wander abroad and lodge in the open air' and was 'not able to give a good account of herself'. For this offence she was sentenced to one month in the House of Correction with hard labour.

Beverley's most famous prisoner to work the treadmill was Robert Peddie who was sentenced, in 1840, to three years imprisonment with hard labour for an attempted Chartist uprising at Bradford. Peddie was an outspoken critic of the treadmill and recorded his feelings in a book called *The Dungeon Harp* published in 1844. While the main purpose of the treadmill was to punish felons through hard physical labour a secondary one was to humiliate them. The building which housed the treadmill was open at one side so that the wheel and the people treading it could be seen from the road running past the prison and, in Peddie's words, 'are daily exposed to gratify the idle curiosity of spectators like wild beasts in a menagerie'.

Peddie's righteous indignation at the humiliation he endured while working the mill meant that he gave a detailed description of its harmful effects. He claimed that the compartments in which the prisoners stood prevented the free circulation of air which 'in warm weather adds much to the prisoners' sufferings' and that after three or four hundred steps the sweat was pouring from him 'like heavy drops in a shower of rain'. Peddie complained bitterly that the rules meant that he had to keep his face turned to the wall because 'turning around to get a mouthful of air is a breach of the regulations which are strictly enforced by an officer placed behind the prisoners, who walks in cloth shoes so as not to be heard by them'. He went on to say that for him the hours he spent working the mill produced giddiness, headaches, nausea and vomiting.

Under the Silent System there seems little doubt that, by the standards of our own day, convicted felons were subject not only to a meagre prison diet, but also to hard demanding labour and to harsh regulations. The system aimed them to make prisoners see the error of their ways and sought to bring about their moral improvement. This meant that the chaplain was a figure of great importance; one of his duties was that of censorship in that he had to 'examine all books proposed to be read by the prisoners'.

In the second half of the nineteenth century the prison system came under the increasing control of national government. Under an act of 1877 the Home Office took control of Beverley's prison and a year later it was closed, the inmates being transferred to West Riding prisons. With the House of Correction now redundant part of it was demolished and another part became the East Riding Police Station and some parts (in Norfolk Street) were converted into private housing. Looking at these picturesque houses today (including the one which housed the treadmill) it is hard to imagine the suffering which Robert Peddie and others endured there over 150 years ago.

23

A Diabolical Crime: The Molescroft Murder

At the height of the First World War, as newspapers focused on the continuing struggle on the Western Front, a crime took place in East Yorkshire that horrified public opinion throughout the United Kingdom. The brutal murder of a thirteen year old girl on a Molescroft farm in February 1917 made national headlines and sickened a nation already hardened to the shedding of innocent blood.

Constitution Hill Farm, lying on the Beverley to Malton road between Molescroft and Cherry Burton, seems an unlikely place for a murder. Set amid a patchwork quilt of fields among rolling hills, the scene today is one of rural tranquillity. In 1917, at a time when motor transport was in its infancy, it would have been quieter still. It was here on Thursday 15 February that the gruesome murder of a thirteen-year old school girl took place.

The facts of the case were well documented in both local and national newspapers of the time. The victim was Lily Tindale, the daughter of John Tindale, a farm bailiff, living at Constitution Hill Farm with his wife and three children. Lily was the youngest of the three sisters and was described as 'a smart well developed girl who looked several years older than her age'. Although she was referred to in the press as a schoolgirl and by her father as a 'bright and good girl', the fact was that Lily was a truant and had not attended St Mary's Girls School in Beverley for about a year before the murder took place. The excuse given for her absence was 'illness brought about through the glands of her neck'.

On Thursday 15 February 1917 Lily had been at work in the farmyard chopping firewood and around 1.30 p.m. had brought an armful of wood into the farmhouse before going out again. This was the last time anyone saw her alive. By around 3 p.m. Mrs Tindale had become alarmed by her daughter's absence and so she sent a message to her husband at work in the fields. A search was then mounted and some time after 4 p.m. John Tindale discovered the body of his daughter in the stackyard of the farm under a pile of loose straw: 'her throat shockingly cut and her clothing covered with blood and dirt'. Strangely, although the stackyard was only one hundred yards from the house no one had heard any screams.

Police Sgt Jackson was later to give evidence that when he arrived at the farm he found the girl on her back and that her clothing was disarranged. Jackson stated that the straw where she lay was saturated with blood and that nearby was part of a razor case but no razor. Evidence from the post-mortem showed that Lily's left eye was 'blackened, bruised and much swollen' and was probably the result of a blow before death. Dr Munro, who had examined the girl,

Constitution Hill Farm, Molescroft.

stated that the clean-cut wound extended across the neck from ear to ear and had divided all the structures from the skin to the spinal column. Munro stated that the wound could not have been self-inflicted. However, despite the obvious savagery of the attack, no medical evidence was produced of sexual assualt.

Suspicion for the murder quickly fell on a shepherd called John Thompson who had gone missing immediately afterwards. Thompson, a single man, had been born at Bewholme near Hornsea and was forty-three years old. The appalling war-time losses of the British Army in France had led to the introduction of conscription and Thompson had been called up for service. However when it was discovered that he was over the legal age requirement the call-up notice had been withdrawn. Thompson had been working at Constitution Hill Farm since May 1916 and with three other farm workers had lived in the farmhouse. He would therefore have come to know Lily Tindale quite well in the six months that followed. Mrs Tindale later said that Thompson had been well behaved during the time he had been on the farm.

On the day of the murder Thompson had, unusually, failed to come into the farmhouse for his dinner and had been seen by Elsie Tindale, Lily's elder sister, walking towards the Molescroft Inn around 12.20 p.m. Margaret Hunsley, the wife of the licensee, was to later report that Thompson had been there, had been served with two pints of beer and had left around 1.00 p.m. She was later to testify that Thompson was quite sober and that she did not notice anything unusual about him. Elsie Tindale went on to state that she had seen Thompson walking towards the stackyard about 1.20 p.m. on that Thursday afternoon.

BRUTAL MURDER ON A YORKSHIRE FARM

Little Girl of Thirteen the Victim.

The brutal murder and mutilation of a 13-year-old girl were described in Beverley Police Court yesterday, when John William Thompson, 42, a shepherd, was charged with the crime and remanded for a week.

The victim was Lucy Tindale, the daughter of John Tindale, of Constitution Hill Farm, where the accused worked.

The father of the girl between his sobs related how he was called from his work in the fields because his daughter was missing. He searched the farm buildings and plantation and eventually found her body in a straw yard buried beneath some straw. Her throat was cut and near by was a part of a razor case said to belong to the prisoner, upon whom suspicion fell, as he had left his sheep and the farm.

The evidence of Police-Sergeant Jackson showed that the girl had made a terrible struggle for life. She was lying on straw saturated with blood. Her body had been mutilated.

Above: Beverley, where Thompson was arrested on the evening of the 15 February 1917.

Left: An account of the murder in the *Weekly Dispatch* newspaper.

Opposite: The Molescroft Inn where John Thompson spent some time before the murder.

Police suspicions about Thompson led to a man hunt in Beverley where it was known that he had relatives. That same evening, armed with a description of the suspect, Detective James Bayley saw Thompson in Beverley's Walkergate and arrested him. The most damning evidence against Thompson at the time of his arrest was his bloodstained hands and clothes. Upon examination Thompson's trousers were so soaked with blood that his knees were stained with it. There was also blood on his clay pipe, his pocket knife and between the fingers of his hands. When told of the murder Thompson was said to have shown a 'callous indifference' and, asked to explain the blood stains on his clothing, claimed he had been bleeding sheep.

Charged with murder and undefended, Thompson appeared in front of East Riding magistrates 'with his hands clasped in front of him and his head bowed; the picture of dejection'. Appearing for the prosecution Deputy Chief Constable Crisp questioned Lily's father about the prisoner's claims that he had been bleeding sheep and established that no sheep had been bled by or in the presence of Thompson that day. Satisfied that there was a case to answer Thompson was remanded in custody and removed to Hedon Road Prison in Hull to await further court appearances.

In the meantime, as the police searched for further evidence of Thompson's guilt, the funeral of Lily Tindale took place in Beverley's Queensgate cemetery on Monday 19 February. A large crowd gathered to witness the white coffin covered in wreaths being lowered into the ground.

When Thompson next appeared before magistrates at the end of February the investigating officer Sgt Jackson was able to report that the murder weapon, Thompson's razor, had been found in a field some distance from the farm. Jackson also testified that near the body of Lily Tindale he had found some footprints (which corresponded with the nails on Thompson's boots) and that on following these footprints they had led him to the razor concealed under a hedge by grass and dead leaves. One of Thompson's co-workers, Robert Quantral, was able to confirm that the razor belonged to Thompson and had been missing from the kitchen mantelpiece, where it was kept, on the day of the murder.

With the committal proceedings over Thompson was sent for trial to the York Assizes where he appeared in front of Judge McCardie on the 9 March 1917. The case took less than one day. Thompson, being a poor shepherd, could not afford representation and so the judge asked Mr Paley Scott to defend him. Mr E. Shortt, KC, MP, appeared for the prosecution and quickly established the overwhelming evidence indicating Thompson's guilt including the fact the stains found on his clothes were human blood. The only chance that Mr Paley Scott had in saving his client from the gallows was to convince the jury that Thompson was insane. He argued that Thompson's actions, in view of the extraordinary ferocity involved in slaying Lily Tindale in such a brutal fashion and his apparent unconcern after the crime, indicated he was suffering from homicidal mania. However, his arguments failed to sway the jury who, after only nineteen minutes deliberation, found Thompson guilty of wilful murder. Judge McCreadie too showed no hesitation when he sentenced him to death by hanging. Thompson, who had maintained an attitude of stolid indifference throughout, took the sentence calmly and was hurried away. He was then sent to Armley Prison in Leeds to await his fate.

In accordance with the law, the customary three Sundays were allowed to elapse before the sentence was carried out. From contemporary newspaper reports it seems that Thompson gave the Armley Prison authorities no trouble. Under the care of the prison chaplain, the Revd Ernest Nuttall, it is said that he made a full confession to his crime. On Tuesday 27 March 1917, at 9 a.m., he walked the few yards from the condemned cell to the gallows where Thomas Pierrepoint, the hangman, and his assistant stood waiting. It is said that Thompson showed no nervousness as his arms and legs were pinioned and the hood and noose were placed over his head. As the prison bell tolled the hour Pierrepoint released the trap and Thompson plunged to his death at the end of the rope. After Thompson's body was left to hang for the customary one hour he was buried in an unmarked grave within the confines of the prison.

To a modern-day observer of these events of 1917 one of the most striking features of the Molescroft Murder case was the speed of early twentieth century justice. From the day of the murder (15 February) to the day of Thompson's execution (27 March) only a mere forty days elapsed; a century later the due process of law might take up to one year or longer. Yet, given the overwhelming body of evidence against Thompson, and his own confession, it would seem that justice was done.

What remains unclear is Thompson's motive for murdering Lily Tindale. Newspaper reports from 1917 are frustratingly silent on the issue; one Beverley edition of March 1917 stated that 'the little girl for no apparent motive but a brutal one was found with her throat cut'. In addition, the evidence of Thompson's guilt, presented to the courts, was so overwhelming that there was no need to establish a motive for his crime while his defence counsel thought his only hope lay in a plea of insanity rather than a plea of mitigation based on the circumstances. Any explanation of Thompson's crime must therefore be speculative. The nature and extent of his relationship with Lily Tindale was never revealed at the time or since and her family would have been anxious to protect the girl's reputation. If the murder of the mature thirteen year-old Lily Tindale by the forty-three year-old John Thompson was a crime of passion then it was a secret that her grieving family kept to themselves.

24

A Passage over the River Hull: Wawne Ferry

River ferries were once a commonplace method of travel in the East Riding. Until the nineteenth century the River Hull between Hull and Tickton (near Beverley) had only two bridges and the way to cross the river was often to use one of the host of river ferries.

In an age before bridges, or when bridges were few in number, river ferries were a vital link in the road network of East Yorkshire. It was the coming of the motorcar that, more than any other factor, sounded the death knell of this ancient mode of transport. Of the many river ferries operating over the River Hull, Wawne Ferry was one of the more famous and long lasting. The ferry was a link in an ancient highway which led from the Roman town of Petuaria (modern-day Brough) to south-eastern Holderness. The ferry replaced a more ancient river crossing: a stone paved ford joining Thearne on the west bank of the River Hull with Wawne on the east bank. We know that the ferry was already in existence by the early twelfth century for in 1136 William le Gros, an important local landowner, gave this 'passage over the River Hull' to the Cistercian Abbey of Meaux which lay close by.

For the first four hundred years of its eight hundred yeas of recorded history the ferry was owned by the monks. The abbey, during the Middle Ages, was a major wool-producer in East Yorkshire. The growth of the market town of Beverley and the rise of its wool manufacturing industry helps to explain the importance of Wawne Ferry which linked the abbey's sheep farms with the spinners and weavers of Beverley. The ferry survived both the decline of Beverley's woollen industry in the later Middle Ages and the dissolution of the monasteries during 1536-1540 when ownership of Wawne Ferry was transferred, for about ninety years, to the crown. During the English Civil Wars of 1642-1646 the ferry played a part in thwarting attempts of the turncoat Governor of Hull, Sir John Hotham, to escape the clutches of his former Parliamentary friends. On June 29 1643 Hotham fled from Hull and attempted to use Wawne Ferry to escape across the River Hull into Holderness. Arriving at the Thearne bank of the river Hotham found that the ferryboat had proceeded upriver. Forced to try and make his escape through the streets of Beverley he was recognised and arrested by the Parliamentary commander there, Colonel Boynton.

In due course the ferry passed under the control of the lords of the manor of Wawne, the Windham family, who continued to own this important river crossing until 1911. For much of its history Wawne Ferry was a simple boat or punt which, because of the shallow nature of the River Hull at this point, would have been 'poled' across the 45ft stretch of water. This pole, called a stour, was about 10ft long and generations of ferrymen learned how to judge the fickle tides

The Windham Arms public house with ferryman Donald Brewer standing in a punt next to the chain-operated pontoon ferry, *c.* 1910.

and undercurrents of the River Hull to propel the boat across. However, there were occasional mishaps and an account book held in the East Riding Archive in Beverley records how in January 1780 the ferryboat sank. On January 26 1780 the Windhams had to pay 12s 0d for 'raising the ferryboat from the bottom of the river'. A local boat builder called William Wiseman from Hull was asked to build a new ferryboat and was paid £60 for the work. The account book also records that when the new ferryboat was first launched in July 1780 the celebrations were marked with the spending of 8s 0d on ale!

Like many ferrymen of the nineteenth and twentieth centuries those operating Wawne Ferry combined this with other work, often inn-keeping or farming. On the eastern side of the river stood the ferryman's home: the Wawne Passage House, built around 1780, and a 33-acre farm which went with the tenancy. By the early nineteenth century the ferryman's home was also a public house and we have more evidence, in the form of local directories and census returns, on those living there. Dominant among the ferrymen in the later nineteenth and twentieth centuries were members of the Brewer family. By 1879 James Brewer, born in Little Weighton, was the ferryman and the 1881 census shows us that he had twelve children. His eldest daughter, Alice, married John Wood of Wawne and Wood became the ferryman in 1895. At an early stage in his tenancy he was to show great courage when he prevented a suicide at the ferry crossing. In May 1895 Wood went into the river to rescue a middle-aged Hull woman called Emily Cousens who was trying to drown herself.

Operating the ferry was not without its difficulties and in the 1880s these seem to have been made worse by the dredging of the river and the removal of the 'Wawne Ferry ridge'. On the 15 October 1885 Edward Knox, agent for the Windhams, wrote a letter to the river authorities complaining about the effects of this dredging on the operation of the ferry and stating 'you have made it impossible to work the ferry boat at low water'. Knox claimed that the work had made it difficult for passengers to use the landing stages of the ferry. By threatening litigation the Windhams were able to secure compensation for new slipways at both the Thearne and Wawne sides of the river and to buy a new chain-operated pontoon ferry.

By about 1890 this new ferry craft was in place and was hauled manually across the river by chains fastened securely to both riverbanks. The chain was pulled hand-over-hand sailor fashion

The riverbanks have been raised since the ferry closed (2003).

in order to draw the pontoon from the Wawne slipway to the Thearne side. The pontoon ferry was large enough to transport animals (including the horses and foxhounds of the Holderness Hunt), farm machinery and cars and was particularly useful at high tide when, because of the dredging operations, working the punt in the deeper water was more difficult. However, there could be mishaps with the pontoon too and on the 10 June 1899 a horse and trap on its way from Beverley to Sutton ended up in the river. Two gentlemen got a soaking and the horse was drowned.

Continuing the family tradition James Brewer's son, Donald Brewer, took over as ferryman in 1909 and two years later he bought the ferry, the farm and the Windham Arms for £2,100 when all were sold at auction by the Windham family. Sales particulars from 1911 show that the takings from the ferry at that time were only £52 per year although combined with the profits from the public house and the farm they would have provided a reasonable income. Donald Brewer was to continue operating the ferry until almost the time it closed charging foot passengers 1d, cyclists 2d and the owners of small cars 6d for each crossing over the river. Passengers arriving at the Thearne side of the river had to ring a bell or shout 'boat' to get his attention.

Although the rise of the motor vehicle at first provided increased opportunities for the ferry in the long term they were the cause of its downfall. With the rise of motorised road transport came pressure for road improvements and the building of more bridges. In July 1937 a new bridge over the River Hull was opened on the newly constructed Sutton Road. Since this was only three miles south of Wawne Ferry any use of the pontoon for transporting vehicles declined rapidly. Although local agricultural contractors, like Mark Jackson of Thearne, occasionally used it to move a tractor to the Wawne side, the regular use of the pontoon effectively ceased leaving mainly the punt to ferry foot passengers and cyclists during the years of the Second World War. The end of the ferry finally came in the summer of 1946 when the Windham Arms, its land and the ferry rights were sold to the Hull-based brewery firm of Moors and Robsons for £3,000. They appointed an elderly man called Walter Twidale as tenant of the Windham Arms and complaints were soon being voiced that he was no longer operating the ferry.

Prominent among the protestors was Ronald Dixon, tenant of Thearne Hall and chairman of Woodmansey Parish Council. By December 1946 Dixon had written to Moors and Robsons

A Humber Keel passing in front of Wawne Ferry, *c.* 1910.

to ask why the ferry had stopped running. He was told that the ferryboat was no longer safe to use and that the cost of repairing or replacing it was not justified by the demand for the service. Dixon fought hard to get the ferry reinstated by raising the matter with the Beverley Rural District Council and with the East Riding County Council but to no avail.

Despite a thorough investigation of the issues involved and pressure by the East Riding of Yorkshire County Council the ferry remained permanently closed after August 1946. The fate of Wawne Ferry was not unique in this respect. The late 1940s were a time of crisis for river ferries and the government's concern was shown by a major investigation of ferries during 1947–1948 by the Ministry of Transport. This study showed that of thirteen pontoon and chain ferries of the type used at Wawne only five were still operating. The typical financial problems of Britain's smaller river ferries in the late 1940s are well illustrated by their investigations into the Stixwould Ferry in Lincolnshire. Here the ferry had been bought by Kesteven Council in 1937. However, such was the decline in ferry traffic that by 1945 they were in the unenviable position of paying someone £2 10s 0d a week to operate the ferry and allowing them to keep the ferry tolls of 7s 0d a week! In these circumstances it is not surprising that Moors and Robsons Ltd denied that they were responsible for maintaining a public ferry service at Wawne.

Some local residents continued to agitate for the resumption of the ferry or for the building of a bridge to replace it into the 1950s. In fact a bridge scheme was nothing new. As early as 1767 the replacement of Wawne Ferry by a bridge had been proposed as part of a new turnpike trust scheme to link the Hull to Beverley turnpike with roads to the east of the river Hull. In the event the scheme came to nothing and Wawne Ferry continued as before.

During both the First and Second World Wars temporary military bridges, to allow for troop movements over the river, were built by the Royal Engineers close to the ferry crossing. In 1919 and again in 1945 the County Council was asked if it wished to buy these bridges for civilian use but on both occasions declined the offer. This is not surprising since these flimsy wooden structures were not really a permanent solution to the problem of bridging the river at Wawne, nor could the narrow lanes have coped with the traffic had a civilian bridge been built. In any case such arguments have now been rendered superfluous by the building of the Ennerdale Bridges downriver from Wawne and serving to open up Hull's newest suburb, Kingswood.

Right: The Holderness Hunt being transported across the River Hull from Thearne to Wawne.

Below: The Ennerdale bridges downstream from the Wawne crossing comprise a pair of single leaf bascule spans, one for each carriageway and have served to open up Hull's newest suburb, Kingswood.

Over fifty years on from the closure of Wawne Ferry, very little remains to remind us of its existence other than the names 'Ferry Lane' on the Thearne side and 'Ferry Road' on the Wawne side of the River Hull. Even the Windham Arms no longer exists, closing its doors for the final time in March 1967. However, the original eighteenth-century Wawne Passage House remains as a private residence and is a lasting tribute to the tradition of 'paying the ferryman'!

25

The Railway That Never Was: The North Holderness Light Railway

As traffic congestion on the A1079 Beverley to York road becomes more serious each day campaigners aim to re-open the Beverley to York Railway. Just over a hundred years ago the people of Beverley and surrounding areas were similarly excited by plans for a new railway line to link the town with the remoter parts of Holderness.

Today's rail travellers waiting at Beverley will, if they are observant, notice a piece of memorabilia close to the northbound platform of the station. Just over a hundred years ago, when Beverley station was part of the North Eastern Railway, a tile map was placed on the station wall showing the extensive railway network owned by that company in East Yorkshire and further afield. Many of these lines were to close in the 1960s during the Beeching cuts including the Hull-Hornsea, Hull-Withernsea and Malton-Driffield railways. More curiously, however, the tile map shows a railway which, though planned, was never actually built: the Beverley to North Frodingham line which would serve *en route* the villages of Tickton, Routh, Long Riston, Leven and Brandesburton.

Although by 1890 railways were widespread many country areas, including large parts of the East Riding, still lacked rail communication. The expense involved in securing an Act of Parliament to authorise a railway and the construction costs needed to meet strict government safety rules were often too great for the likely financial returns. To expand the benefits of railways to rural areas at lesser cost, therefore, Parliament passed the Light Railways Act in 1896. This cheapened the process of getting approval for a railway, lessened construction costs by allowing level crossings across main roads instead of embankments and bridges and relaxed the safety rules in return for strict speed restrictions (20 mph). By the end of that year a series of plans had been tabled for several light railways in rural East Yorkshire. At a meeting in Brandesburton (15 January 1896), for example, a proposal was discussed for a light railway from Beverley to Hornsea with a branch to Beeford from Leven. However, of the schemes discussed, the one that came closest to being realized was the North Holderness Light Railway Company's plan for a 12 mile single track railway linking Beverley and North Frodingham.

Prime movers in the scheme were country gentlemen, like Captain William Preston of Leven and Major James Harrison of Brandesburton Hall, although they also sought to draw in the support of parish councils, Beverley Corporation, the East Riding County Council and the North Eastern Railway. According to one of the promoters, William Preston, the idea was to have 'no luxuries' and to have the line built 'as cheaply as possible'. To lessen costs the Light

One of the promoters of the new railway was Col. James Harrison of Brandesburton Hall.

Railway Regulations allowed the Company to take up and set down passengers at any place on the railway without providing stations or platforms. William Preston told Leven Parish Council in March 1897 that three or four engines would be needed at a cost of £400 each while eleven level crossings would have to be constructed at £40 each. The cost of small station platforms at places like Tickton was put at £70 each. From the outset the promoters realized that economies would give their plans a greater chance of success. In their original plans the Beverley terminus of the new railway was to be in a field to the east of Beverley Station where two acres of land was set aside for a passenger station, goods depot, sidings, engine sheds and a turntable. However, Captain Preston acknowledged that if the NER could be persuaded to allow the use of the existing Beverley station economies of £500 could be achieved. The engineer for the light railway, George Bohn of Hull, estimated that the total cost of the scheme would be about £30,000 At the public enquiry into the new railway, held by the Light Railway Commissioners at Beverley in early October 1897, Bohn suggested that the flat nature of the terrain meant that there would be no great engineering difficulties to hinder construction.

However, in common with many new railway schemes this new line had its opponents. A newspaper report of May 1897 records that a meeting of the principal residents of Routh disapproved of the new railway on the grounds that 'it was not required'. At the October public enquiry counsel for the largest landowner affected by the plans, William Bethell declared, correctly as it turned out, that 'the railway would never succeed'. However, since Bethell was the owner of the Leven Canal and his business would be badly affected by the new line, his opinion was hardly impartial! Most of those present at the enquiry, however, supported the proposals

In September 1903 three new motor omnibuses purchased by the NER launched the Beverley-North Frodingham service. The photograph shows two of the buses waiting at the Black Swan Inn, Brandesburton. (courtesy Beverley Local Studies Library)

including many local farmers (who were attracted by the prospect of moving agricultural produce at less cost), county, town and parish councils, the Beverley Traders' Association and the firm of Cochrane and Cooper. The latter were active in building steam trawlers on the River Hull at Grovehill and claimed, extravagantly, that the firm would put 5,000 tons of traffic on the railway each year. The plans for North Holderness Light Railway included a goods depot and station at Grovehill to serve the needs of industry along the River Hull.

Beverley Corporation was anxious for the scheme to go ahead not only because they believed that it would help the economy of the town but also because they had an agreement with the railway company that the bridge over the River Hull at Grovehill would be dual purpose. As well as carrying the single track railway it would also provide for road vehicles and pedestrians thereby replacing the ancient Grovehill Ferry. In return for their contribution to the cost of construction the Corporation intended charging tolls on those using it (for foot passengers a half-penny and for two-wheeled horse drawn vehicles, two pence).

Having listened to the arguments, for and against, the Light Railway Commissioners approved the construction of the new railway in early 1898. With the formalities complete the construction of the line should then have commenced. In January 1898 George Bohn recommended that the company should appoint, as contractors, Sangwins of Hull. According to Bohn, Sangwins had done a large amount of work for him previously and had never been known 'to attempt any of the usual contractor's frauds'. Yet, despite all these preparations no work was done; it seems likely that the North Holderness Company could not raise the necessary cash to build the line.

Beverley Railway Station was planned to be the terminus of the new North Holderness Light Railway to North Frodingham.

The scheme was, however, by no means dead for by December 1898 the North Eastern Railway (NER) was actively seeking powers to build the line instead and gained permission under an act of 1899.

With the financial resources of a large railway company behind the scheme there should, in theory, have been no further delay. According to later reports the NER did buy up most of the land that was needed for the railway and they also drew up plans for the carriages and trucks to be used. However, there was no progress on the ground. Beverley Corporation's involvement with the new Grovehill Bridge meant that they were anxious to see the scheme commence. When, in February 1900, councillors began to ask when the building of the line would begin. Alderman Turner optimistically suggested that 'it would be commenced at an early date'. Despite some disagreement with the NER over the Corporation's share of the cost of the Grovehill Bridge (March 1900) there was no indication, at this stage, that the scheme was to be abandoned. Detailed drawings of the new railway (for example, of the location of the new Swinemoor Lane level-crossing gatehouse) dated 30 August 1900 show that the company was still pressing ahead with its plans. Yet as the year 1900 drew to a close it became obvious that the company's schedule was going seriously awry. On 15 December 1900 at a meeting of the Beverley Town Council, Cllr Dugglesby asked if there was any likelihood of the light railway ever being constructed. Cllr Millett told the meeting that he had been informed that there was no possibility of the light railway being started during the winter of 1900-1901. However, it was not until a year later, in December 1901, that the NER formally abandoned their plans when they wrote to Beverley

Corporation to say they had decided 'not to proceed with the construction of the railway'. This announcement was met with both disappointment and anger; the town clerk was told to write to the NER expressing the Corporation's 'regret' that the railway company had not carried out their obligations. A letter-writer to a local newspaper meanwhile was more forthright in his criticism. On 21 December 1901 he declared that it was 'the most shameful and scandalous betrayal of the public by a railway company I ever heard of'.

Why then did the NER abandon their plans for the North Holderness Light Railway? There seems little doubt that the company was in earnest in wanting to build the line and had already spent considerable sums in preparation for it. They had obtained, by act of Parliament, the power to take over the plans of the North Holderness Light Railway Company, had bought much of the land over which the railway would run, had designed carriages and trucks for it and had shown their intention to run such a railway by including it on new tile maps of the NER system (like the one in Beverley station). The main reason, it seems, for their change of heart was that the new light railway no longer made good business sense. Before they abandoned the scheme the NER had already modified it by providing alternative proposals for a cheaper narrow gauge railway. Engineering drawings from the North Eastern Railway's York offices show two different kinds of narrow gauge rolling stock designed to run on a 2ft wide track. These changes would have made the railway cheaper to build and to equip. In the end the NER decided against building any kind of railway claiming that this was due 'to the cost coming out at a figure very largely in excess of the estimate'.

By 1901 the NER had probably realised that substituting a motor bus service for the light railway would make more economic sense. The country's first motor buses had been built in 1898 and the NER seems to have believed that these would be a more cost effective alternative to the North Holderness Light Railway. In September 1903 three new motor omnibuses purchased by the NER launched the Beverley-North Frodingham service. Built by the Scottish engineering firm of Stirlings they could carry sixteen passengers inside and half a ton of luggage on the roof at an average speed of 12 mph! One of the guests on the trial run of Monday 31 August 1903 was Major Harrison, the originator of the light railway scheme. According to newspaper reports of the event he and the other guests expressed themselves 'delighted with the new service'.

The North Holderness Light Railway, therefore, became the railway that never was. With the benefit of hindsight, it could be argued that the NERs decision in abandoning it was the correct one. The history of East Yorkshire's rural branch lines in the twentieth century was one of decline and closure and there seems little doubt that the fate of the Beverley to North Frodingham line would have been the same. Furthermore, today's motorists plagued by the frequent delays at Beverley's notorious level crossings will be pleased by the fact that the one destined to carry the new railway over Swinemoor Lane was never built!

26

A Victorian White Elephant: The Hull and Barnsley Railway

As today's motorists enter Hull along the city's notoriously congested Beverley Road they pass under a railway bridge carrying freight traffic to the eastern docks. Some modern-day observers have suggested that this dock's railway might be the answer to Hull's traffic needs in the twentieth century since it could form the basis of a congestion-beating passenger network. If these proposals ever come into being the people of Hull will have cause to thank a group of dynamic, if misguided, businessmen and civic leaders who, in the 1870s were determined that the city should have new railway links to the west.

The growth of Hull had begun long before the arrival of railways. From the late eighteenth century the town had been able to expand beyond the confines of its medieval fortifications: first with the building of the Old Dock (later Queens Dock) and later with other docks forming a ring around the Old Town. Hull's first railway, opened in 1840, linked the port with the West Riding via Selby. This soon became part of the North Eastern Railway and because this had a monopoly of rail traffic in the East Riding many Hull businessmen believed there was need for an independent line to break their stranglehold.

The criticisms of the NER became louder during the trade boom of 1872 when the inadequacies of Hull's railway and dock facilities became apparent with a complete traffic breakdown. As a result of the chaos a scheme for a new railway and dock was proposed at the end of 1872. This Hull, South and West Junction Railway, it was suggested, would have a tunnel under the Humber and link up with one of the NER's rivals at Brigg in Lincolnshire. However, largely because of concerns about the Humber railway tunnel, the bill was rejected by the House of Lords.

The arguments that Hull needed better rail and dock provision would not, however, go away and found a champion in Gerard Smith, a Hull banker. In 1879 plans were begun for an independent railway to the South Yorkshire coalfield and a new dock on the Humber foreshore. These proposals were supported by a number of Hull's leading merchants and industrialists, as well as Hull Corporation. Despite the opposition of the NER and the Hull Dock Company an act of parliament approving the Hull, Barnsley and West Riding Junction Railway and Dock Company was passed in August 1880. The approval of the new railway and dock was met with great rejoicing in Hull with processions, music and firework displays.

Work on building the new railway began almost at once with Gerard Smith performing the ceremony of 'turning the first sod' at the site of the new dock on Hedon Road (15 January 1881). The firm of Lucas and Aird had been appointed as contractors for the railway and dock and they

The bridge over Beverley Road, 2006. The name of the pub under the arches, Cannon Junction, recalls the days when at this point on the Hull and Barnsley Railway the line branched. One line continued to Alexandra Dock and the other to the passenger terminus at Cannon Street.

soon commenced work on both. The railway began at Alexandra Dock and encircled the town on an embankment; near Beverley Road it was joined by a short branch from the passenger terminus. The line climbed out of Hull through the chalk ridge of the Wolds before reaching the Vale of York and then the coal bearing lands between Barnsdale Bar and Cudworth. The line took just over four years to build but was hindered, from the outset, by an underestimate of construction costs. The Act of 1880 had made provision for a capital of £3,000,000 (in £10 shares) and further borrowing powers of £1,000,000. In the event, the railway cost twice as much as had been estimated and at £101,900 per mile was one of the most expensive ever constructed. A major factor in this overspend was the difficulty of constructing the line through the hard chalk of the wolds where explosives were often necessary to excavate cuttings tunnels (eg. Drewton Tunnel is over a mile in length).

Much of the work was done by navvies using picks and shovels and in 1883 alone there were 4,000 of them at work on the railway. Most worked from dawn to dusk for six days a week and were paid a weekly wage of about 30 shillings for this back-breaking labour. The work was also dangerous and accidents were not uncommon. The first fatal accident was to a seventy year old navvy working on an embankment in the Hull area who was buried under a fall of earth. Limited use was also made of mechanical excavators; three steam navvies were used to excavate cuttings on the railway. As the material from the Wolds was excavated wagon loads of it were moved to Hull to form embankments around the city.

The financial crises of the Hull and Barnsley Railway meant that economies had to be made from the outset and plans for a fine new passenger terminus for Hull (to be built at Kingston Square, near the New Theatre) were abandoned before the railway opened. Instead, a much less convenient location was chosen at Cannon Street where a carriage shed was altered to create a passenger terminus.

In fact, despite the extravagant claims of the company, in its 1880 prospectus, that: 'a valuable suburban traffic might be conveniently looked for' passenger receipts for the railway were never great. The railway opened to passenger traffic on the 27 July 1885 and the last passenger train (from Howden to Hull) ran on the 30 July 1955. This was almost ten years before the 'Beeching Axe' cut a swathe through other rural train services in the East Riding (like the Hull and

Above: The Hull and Barnsley Railway was expensive to build because of the difficult terrain it passed through. Tunnels, cuttings and viaducts (like the one shown here at Eppleworth near Cottingham) were costly undertakings. (courtesy Nick Cox)

Below: Excursion trains on the Hull and Barnsley Railway.

HULL & BARNSLEY RAILWAY.

Every Thursday and Saturday,

Until Further Notice,

COOK'S CHEAP DAY EXCURSIONS TO

SHEFFIELD,

With Bookings on Saturdays for **2** or **3** days.

From	dep.	dep.	To SHEFFIELD. Day Trip Fare.	To SHEFFIELD. 2 or 3 Days on Saturdays only.
	a.m.	a.m.		
HULL—				
Cannon Street	7 0	9 40	**2/9**	**4/9**
Beverley Road	7 4	9 44		
HOWDEN	7 50	10 24		
Sheffield ... ... arr.	9 22	11 45		

The Return Train will leave Sheffield at 6-58 p.m. or 8-28 p.m. each day.

Passengers taking tickets at the higher fares must return by ordinary train leaving Sheffield at 6-58 p.m. or 8-28 p.m. on Week-days, and on Sundays at 3-34 p.m.

Every Thursday, Saturday and Sunday,

Until further notice, Cook's Cheap Return Tickets to

LITTLE WEIGHTON, SOUTH CAVE & NORTH CAVE,

Available to return from either Station on day of issue; and to

DRAX and KIRK SMEATON,

Will be issued as under:—

FROM	Times of Starting. Week-Days.			Times of Starting. Sundays.	Return Fares, Third Class. LITTLE WEIGHTON, SOUTH CAVE and NORTH CAVE.	Return Fares, Third Class. DRAX.	Return Fares, Third Class. KIRK SMEATON.
HULL—	p.m.	p.m.	p.m.	By any ordinary stopping train in each direction.	Third Class.	Third Class.	Third Class.
Cannon Street ...	12 30	1 25	3 0		**1/-**	**1/3**	**1/9**
Beverley Road ...	12 34	1 29	3 4				

NOTE.—Bookings to Drax and Kirk Smeaton by 12·20 p.m. train. Bookings to Little Weighton, South and North Cave, by any of the three trains named.

BICYCLES.—Bicycle Tickets, at owner's risk are issued to Excursionists from Hull to **KIRK SMEATON** at **1/-** each return when properly labelled.

Children under 3 years of age, free: above 3 and under 12, half fares. The tickets are not transferable, and are available by the trains herein-named only. No luggage allowed to passengers taking day or half-day trip tickets. Passengers holding long-date tickets are allowed 60 lbs. of luggage free, under their own care, for which the Company will not be responsible.

NOTE.—The Tickets are only available to and from the Stations named above, and passengers alighting at any other Station will forfeit their tickets and be required to pay the full ordinary fare.

Should the Company consider it necessary or desirable, from any cause, to alter or cancel these arrangements, they reserve to themselves the right to do so.

Springhead Halt was built on the Hull boundary to boost passenger receipts but it failed to do so. (courtesy Nick Cox)

Hornsea line) and reflects the moribund state of passenger traffic even from the village stations closest to Hull like Willerby and Little Weighton.

Freight traffic on the Hull and Barnsley was generally more successful than passenger services, particularly the coal trade. Traffic was at an all time high in 1913 when mineral receipts alone totalled almost £400,000 and the main line between Springhead sidings in Anlaby and Sandholme was frequently carrying a hundred trains a day in each direction. However in the years of the First World War and the 1920s there was a steady decline in the coal, mineral and freight traffic carried.

The independent life of the Hull and Barnsley railway came to an end in March 1922 when it was amalgamated with its old rival the North Eastern Railway (soon to be the LNER). However, the decline in coal, mineral and freight traffic continued as before. As competition from road freight increased so the number of trains using the Hull and Barnsley route diminished: by 1955, the year in which passenger services ceased, there were only sixteen or seventeen freight trains daily each way over the main line. Furthermore, a recession in the coal and steel industries during 1958 led to a full re-appraisal of the line and the greater part of it through the Wolds was closed. A limited goods service to Little Weighton continued until 1964 when that too ended.

Thus ended the relatively short life of an enterprise which had been greeted in Hull in 1880 with both optimism and enthusiasm. There is little doubt that the railway's chances of success were blighted from the outset by the high cost of building it through difficult terrain as well as over-optimistic forecasts of the traffic it would generate. It could be argued that the earlier scheme of 1872, with its tunnel under the Humber, would have been a cheaper, more viable project in the long term since it would have presented fewer construction difficulties and have brought London 15 miles nearer. Instead, by 1921 over four and a half million pounds had been spent on a railway which became little more than a white elephant. As one historian, writing in 1948 when the line was still largely operational, commented, 'that it played its part in the development of Hull cannot be doubted, but whether its contribution was commensurate with the effort and money expended on it is not so certain'.

27

Wonderful Welton

Although it lies close to the busy A63 trunk road into Hull the village of Welton has managed to retain that same picturesque charm which has endeared it to generations of East Riding folk. Although the name Welton is Saxon the evidence indicates that there was some settlement here during the Iron Age and in Roman times; down the road from Welton is Brough, known in Roman times as Petuaria.

As the name suggests one of the attractions of Welton was a ready supply of water. In East Yorkshire parlance a well is a spring and since it lies at the foot of the Yorkshire Wolds, Welton (the town of Wells) has no shortage of them. One of Welton's most attractive features is the stream that runs through it and laps the churchyard wall as it curves from north to south. The power of this stream once turned a water wheel at a corn mill close to the church. In fact, Welton was so blessed with waterpower that as early as the Domesday Book (1086) three water mills were mentioned. Only one of these remains: the High Mill situated in Welton Dale, a deep picturesque glen winding between two hills to the north of the village. This imposing five-storey mill building housed a gigantic breast-shot waterwheel, nearly 35ft in diameter, working three pairs of stones. The present waterwheel was installed in 1861 at a time when extensive modernisation of the mill was taking place. However, by its very nature, waterpower can sometimes be unreliable (for example during a summer drought) and so in 1904 a paraffin engine was installed to supplement it. By 1914 this had been replaced by a gas engine and finally, before its closure in the 1960s, by electricity.

The high mill may no longer be in use but the attractiveness of its setting, Welton Dale, is still there to lure visitors and walkers as it has been doing for over a century. The great natural beauty of this typical Yorkshire Wolds dry valley has long been a magnet for day-trippers from Hull and further afield. As early as 1892 a local directory urged 'tourists wishing to visit this beautiful dale to obtain a pass from Mr Robinson, farm bailiff, in the village'. Today the idyllic scenery of Welton Dale forms part of the Wolds Way, much loved by walkers and ramblers alike.

At the heart of Welton village stands the parish church of St Helena. Although Welton probably had a wooden church from Saxon times the present stone-built one seems to date from the reign of William Rufus (1087-1100). During restoration of the church in 1863 six silver pennies from this era were discovered in the foundations. St Helena, with its large square central tower and attractive watery setting (complete with ducks), is well worth a look inside too. As well as several windows containing beautiful stained glass there is also an effigy of a Knight Templar to see.

The Knights Templar were an order of crusading knights who fought the Muslims in Palestine but also accumulated great wealth and influence in western Europe during the Middle Ages. In Yorkshire they were active in all kinds of commerce and agriculture until their suppression in 1308. The existence of a large Knight Templar priory at nearby North Ferriby (from about 1200) might also help to explain the effigy in Welton church.

On a headstone outside the church can be seen another unusual memorial from some 500 years later: this time it was to a Welton resident called Jeremiah Simpson who died in 1719, aged 84. According to the inscription:

> Here lieth he, ould Jeremy,
> Who have eight times married been,
> But now in his ould age,
> He lies in his cage,
> Under the grass so green.

Whether the eighteenth-century poet who penned this verse was commenting on Jeremiah's extreme old age (for those times) or his ability to outlive his wives is unclear!

Another highlight of Welton, situated close to the village green, is the historic Green Dragon public house. Originally called the Green Man it is the only one of Welton's three former inns still remaining. According to legend it was here, in October 1738, that the infamous highwayman Dick Turpin was arrested.

One of the interesting features of the Green Dragon is the former stables to be found behind

Right: Near the head of Welton Dale is the Raikes mausoleum, a circular building of stone surmounted by a dome. It was built by the owner of Welton House, Robert Raikes (1765-1837), a prominent Hull banker. The building dates from 1818 and was designed to be the final resting place of Raikes and his family.

Below: The watermill at Welton (Welton High Mill).

Opposite: The beauty of Welton village.

Welton village green. The drinking fountain was placed here in the early nineteenth century and the green was used for the annual village fair.

the inn for it was once a posting house on the coach route from South Cave via Brantingham into Hull. Here weary travellers could obtain refreshment while the exhausted horses were changed for fresh ones.

Improved communications and better roads meant that Welton, by the late eighteenth and early nineteenth centuries, had become a popular place to live among Hull's growing number of wealthy merchants. Many handsome houses were built in the village at this time some of which remain including the stone-built Welton Grange, dating from around 1741. Among those seeking the life of a country gentleman in this desirable location was Robert Raikes (1765-1837), a Hull banker, who lived at Welton House. Such was his influence in the 1830s that he prevented the new Hull and Selby railway from passing through his estates and this meant that Brough, rather than Welton, was chosen as the site for the nearest railway station. A lasting memorial to Robert Raikes can be found in Welton Dale where he built a circular, domed, Roman-style mausoleum for himself and his family.

Another important local family, who occupied Welton House from 1849, were the Broadleys. In the late eighteenth century the banker Robert Carlile Broadley had re-invested his fortune in land around Hull and throughout the East Riding. Such was the success of this strategy that it was said that in the nineteenth century 'a man cannot walk out of Hull in any direction without walking on land at one time or other owned by the Broadley family'. In due course these thousands of acres passed under the control of Robert's bachelor-nephew Henry Broadley and it was he who bought Welton House and made it the centre of his business empire. On his death in 1851 the estate passed to his unmarried sister Sophia. The village had much to thank her for as Sophia provided the £6,000 needed to restore the church in 1863.

By the late nineteenth century her successor, William Harrison, had changed the family name to Harrison-Broadley but his importance in the community was still evident. A local directory from 1892 lists him as one of the magistrates who dispensed justice "every alternate Monday in the courtroom at Welton."

The importance of the Broadley family to Welton continued until around 1944 when the death of J.B. Harrison Broadley led to the sale of the estate in separate lots and opened the way for much post-war development. However, the heart of historic Welton remains to remind twentieth-century visitors of the charm of village life in a bygone age.

28

Gone for a Burton

The study of place names is a fascinating business and can reveal much about the origins of towns and villages. An interesting example of a common place-name in the north is that of Burton - in the East Riding alone there are eight such villages from Burton Fleming in the north to Brandesburton and Burton Pidsea in the south. The word Burh-tun comes to us from the Angles, a Germanic tribe who settled in Eastern England from the fifth century and means a fortified village or farmstead. The need to distinguish between one fortified village and another meant the addition of other words and so we see names like Cherry Burton and Burton Agnes appearing. Thus the name of Burton Agnes, about six miles west of Bridlington, was probably derived from a twelfth-century lady of the manor, Agnes of Aumale. Similarly, the village of Burton Pidsea, east of Hull, gets its name from the mere or lake which once occupied part of the low lying and water logged plain of Holderness close by. Improved land drainage meant that Pidsea Mere had disappeared by the mid seventeenth century although its name lives on through the village.

Just over two miles from Beverley is the delightful village of Cherry Burton (named, it is thought, from cherry trees in the locality). The name itself dates from the fifteenth century even though the settlement was much older. Close to Cherry Burton is one of East Yorkshire's most attractive villages: Bishop Burton. Sitting in a sheltered hollow astride the A1709 this ancient village enjoys well-kept greens, majestic chestnut trees and neat white-washed houses and is a visual delight for residents and visitors alike. Originally known as Burtone the village was, from 1066, part of the estates of the Archbishops of York and acquired its more famous name by its associations with them.

The sites of several 'Burton' villages made them ideal for early habitation being located on rising ground on the edge of the Yorkshire Wolds rather than the lower lying fens and marshes of Holderness. A major advantage of places like Burton Agnes, Cherry Burton and Bishop Burton was easy access to fresh water springs, an important consideration in the days before this vital commodity came on tap. The abundance of water at these sites is shown by a feature common to all three places: village ponds. Bishop Burton has two and the larger one, crescent shaped, is more the size of a lake. It provides a magical vista for the village, especially when approached from the Beverley direction.

The similarity between these East Riding villages does not end with ponds. Bishop Burton, Burton Agnes and Burton Pidsea, for example, all have associations with horse racing. In the eighteenth and nineteenth centuries Yorkshire was a major centre of horse breeding and through

the efforts of Richard Watt (1786-1855) Bishop Burton became famous for the quality of its bloodstock. Watt was the son of a wealthy Liverpool merchant who purchased the High Hall in 1783 (where Bishop Burton College now stands). Watt's horses and harlequin racing colours brought fame to the village, a fact reflected in the various names given to Bishop Burton's public house in the early nineteenth century. In a directory of 1823 it was called Evander after one of Richard Watt's horses; later it became the Horse and Jockey and finally the Altisidora. In 1813 Altisidora had become the first of Richard Watt's horses to win the England's premier horse race of that time, the St Ledger. Watt went on to win three more St Ledgers between 1823 and 1833 with horses called Barefoot, Memnon and Rockingham.

When they died many of Richard Watt's horses, including Altisidora, were buried beneath the parkland surrounding his home with their graves marked by oak trees. Following the death of Richard Watt his son William carried on the business. Today, the Bishop Burton connection with horse racing is kept alive by a bequest of £3,000 to the trustees of Beverley Racecourse to fund the yearly Watt Memorial Race.

Burton Pidsea too has a strong connection with the 'sport of kings' and this is reflected in the name of the village public house, The Nancy Inn. Dating from the mid-eighteenth century, and formerly the site of a blacksmith's forge, The Nancy was named after the successful racehorse bred locally by Edward Baxter which won eleven races in 1851.

The importance of the horse in the rural economy for farm work and transport is also reflected in other pub signs; Cherry Burton, for example, still has its Bay Horse Inn. In an age

Right: The village green of Brandesburton with its ancient stone cross.

Opposite: The larger of Bishop Burton's two ponds.

before motor transport, East Riding villages had to be far more self-sufficient than they are now. A study of village directories for the Burtons in the early part of the nineteenth century reveals a host of trades, now vanished. These were vital both for farming and a self-sufficient community and included shoemakers, tailors, wheelwrights and blacksmiths The blacksmith's forge was an essential part of a largely agricultural economy from shoeing horses to repairing ploughs and all kinds of farm machinery. Until the 1950s the red heat of the blacksmith's fire and the sound of his hammer on the anvil were commonplace in East Riding villages. In Cherry Burton generations of blacksmiths worked a forge situated near the village pond since a ready supply of water was necessary to douse hot metal.

In an age of coaches, carts and other horse-drawn vehicles the wheelwright too was an essential tradesman. The village of Brandesburton on the well-used road from Beverley to Bridlington seems to have been a centre for the building and repair of wagons; a directory of 1823 lists four wheelwrights in the village. Brandesburton was a thriving place with three markets a week, an annual horse fair and even its own horse races. Brandesburton's economy benefited from the considerable traffic through the village in the late eighteenth and early nineteenth centuries as shown by its two coaching inns: the Cross Keys (renamed the Dacre Arms by 1872) and the Black Swan. During the eighteenth century the Cross Keys was reputed to be the largest posting inn of its type in the East Riding providing food, drink and accommodation. It had stabling for fifty horses around a cobbled yard, a jockey room for coachmen to clean and store their harness and its own brewery at a time when the local brewing of ale was still very much the norm.

The Black Swan, Brandesburton.

The inn also had a secret room, accessible only by a trapdoor, which according to legend sheltered fugitives during the 1745 Jacobite Rebellion and was used by smugglers for storing their contraband.

Close to the most picturesque part of Brandesburton, the village green complete with ancient stone cross, was the Black Swan. With a yard and stabling accommodation, the inn was a lively bustling place and a favourite stopping point for coaches and travellers. The inn even had a horseman's window from which a rider could be served without dismounting from his steed. Brandesburton and its old coaching inns suffered from the opening of the Hull and Bridlington Railway in 1846; faster travel by train served to by-pass the old coaching route via Leven and Brandesburton.

The villages of East Yorkshire have probably seen more changes in the last fifty years than in the previous five hundred. In an age of motorised transport these rural gems of yesteryear have became attractive locations for commuters seeking tranquillity from the hustle and bustle of modern life. Villages like Burton Pidsea, Brandesburton and Cherry Burton have attracted significant modern housing development but also the parking problems and traffic congestion that go with it. This may have altered the character of these villages though not necessarily their charm. Through conservation and planning the best features of our historic village past can be preserved for future generations.